Multiple intelligences

... Theme-Based Activities

body wise
bodily–kinesthetic

word wise
verbal–linguistic

logic wise
logical–mathematical

nature wise
naturalist

music wise
musical–rhythmic

people wise
interpersonal

picture wise
visual–spatial

self wise
intrapersonal

www.worldteacherspress.com

Published with the permission of R.I.C. Publications Pty. Ltd.

Copyright © 2005 by Didax, Inc., Rowley, MA 01969. All rights reserved.

First published by R.I.C. Publications Pty. Ltd., Perth, Western Australia. Revised by Didax Educational Resources.

Limited reproduction permission: The publisher grants permission to individual teachers who have purchased this book to reproduce the blackline masters as needed for use with their own students. Reproduction for an entire school or school district or for commercial use is prohibited.

Printed in the United States of America.

Order Number 2-5242
ISBN 1-58324-208-2

A B C D E F 09 08 07 06 05

395 Main Street
Rowley, MA 01969
www.worldteacherspress.com

Foreword

The theory of multiple intelligences places value on a range of eight different learning intelligences—acknowledging individual differences. Teachers and students favor a particular learning style (or styles). This series aims to provide teaching and learning opportunities, using the eight multiple intelligences through a thematic approach in the classroom.

Titles in this series:

Multiple intelligences – Grades 1 to 3
Multiple intelligences – Grades 3 to 5
Multiple intelligences – Grades 6 to 8

Contents

Teacher's notes	iv – vi
How to use this book	vii – viii
Teacher self-assessment worksheet	ix
Assessment of student learning styles worksheet	x – xi
Student self-assessment of learning styles worksheet	xii – xiii

Space (cover page) 1
- Space overview 2–3
- Informational text 4–5
- Planetary poetry 6–7
- Planet facts 8–9
- Stargazing 10–11
- Space travel brochure 12–13
- Fit for space! 14–15
- Space symphony 16–17
- Alien ship 18–19
- Space diary 20–21
- Student self-assessment 22

Water (cover page) 23
- Water overview 24–25
- Informational text 26–27
- Watery poetry 28–29
- Evaporation in a saucer 30–31
- Desert plants and animals 32–33
- Sea monster alert! 34–35
- Cooking demonstration 36–37
- Thunderstorm soundscape 38–39
- Water park design 40–41
- Endangered sea animal 42–43
- Student self-assessment 44

Life cycles (cover page) 45
- Life cycles overview 46–47
- Informational text 48–49
- Life cycle of a frog 50–51
- Growing seeds 52–53
- Our class pet 54–55
- The cycle of life 56–57
- Plan a fitness circuit 58–59
- Jingle – How do you grow? 60–61
- Animal interview 62–63
- Action plan 64–65
- Student self-assessment 66

Festivals (cover page) 67
- Festivals overview 68–69
- Informational text 70–71
- Festival in the news! 72–73
- What's on? 74–75
- The environment celebrates too! 76–77
- What does it represent? 78–79
- Festival mask 80–81
- Rap it out! 82–83
- Festival day 84–85
- Oh! What a feeling! 86–87
- Student self-assessment 88

Good health (cover page) 89
- Good health overview 90–91
- informational text 92–93
- Why drink? 94–95
- Nutrition information 96–97
- Our health and the environment 98–99
- Healthy food posters 100–101
- An active life 102–103
- Jingle – Selling good health 104–105
- Party menu 106–107
- Food and my body 108–109
- Student self-assessment 110

Dinosaurs (cover page) 111
- Dinosaurs overview 112–113
- Informational text 114–115
- Lizard-hipped and bird-hipped dinosaurs 116–117
- Dinosaur environments 118–119
- Dinosaur dig 120–121
- Swinging dinosaurs 122–123
- Prehistoric fun and games 124–125
- Dinosaur rap 126–127
- Theme party – Dinosaur style 128–129
- Dinosaur hunt 130–131
- Student self-assessment 132

Teacher's notes

What is "multiple intelligences"?

The theory of multiple intelligences was developed by psychologist Dr. Howard Gardner after years of biological and cultural research into human cognition.

In his 1983 book, *Frames of mind: the theory of multiple intelligences*, Gardner suggests that there are seven (later eight) different types of human intelligence or ways of understanding the world—and possibly even more yet to be identified. This idea is in contrast to the traditional view of intelligence, where it is thought of as a general characteristic that affects our skills and abilities. IQ tests are a perfect example of this latter belief.

Gardner believes that each person has one or two dominant intelligences, although it is possible to strengthen all eight. He points out that our intelligences aren't used in isolation; instead, one activity or task requires the use of a number of intelligences working together.

The eight intelligences identified by Gardner are verbal–linguistic, logical–mathematical, naturalist, visual–spatial, bodily–kinesthetic, musical–rhythmic, interpersonal, and intrapersonal. Typical characteristics of a student with a dominance in an intelligence and suitable activities for developing or assessing each intelligence are outlined below. Each of these intelligences is also described on the teacher page preceding each worksheet.

To make the terminology easier for the students to understand, the terms have been simplified with an accompanying icon for each intelligence.

Intelligence		Activities involving ...
Verbal–Linguistic A student who thinks in words. He/She learns best through activities involving reading, writing, and speaking.		verbal and written communication, vocabulary, word puzzles and games, spelling, listening to people speak or read aloud
Logical–Mathematical A student who thinks rationally and in abstractions. He/She learns best through activities involving numbers and patterns.		problem-solving, brainteasers, logical puzzles, questioning how things work, science experiments, number games or problems, complex ideas
Naturalist A student with an awareness of the patterns in nature. He/She learns best through activities involving animals, plants, and the environment.		gardening, animals and plants, observing and identifying environmental features
Visual–Spatial A student who thinks in images, colors and shapes. He/She learns best through activities involving visualization.		art, crafts and design, watching movies, interpreting images, visual puzzles or games
Bodily–Kinesthetic A student with good physical awareness. He/She learns best through "hands-on" activities.		craft, motor coordination, sports skills, acting, demonstrations, taking objects apart and putting them back together
Musical–Rhythmic A student with an awareness of rhythm and sound. He/She learns best through activities involving music or rhythms.		playing musical instruments, singing, rhythm, identification of sounds, interpreting music, chants
Interpersonal A student who enjoys being in groups and teams. He/She learns best through activities involving working with others.		friendship qualities, being a leader, playing team sports, group work, and showing empathy for others
Intrapersonal A student who understands and analyzes his/her thoughts and feelings. He/She learns best through individual activities.		identifying beliefs, expressing feelings, working alone, personal challenges, setting and reaching goals

Teacher's notes

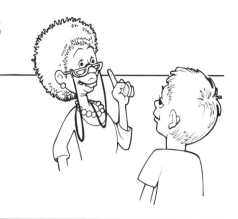

Implications of multiple intelligences for teaching

In the traditional western education system, a student's intelligence is largely measured by his/her linguistic and mathematical abilities. This undervalues abilities and achievements in other curriculum areas. The theory of multiple intelligences, in contrast, values equally a range of different intelligences and thereby acknowledges individual differences. If teachers accept Gardner's theory, it has implications for the way they plan, present, and assess student work.

Setting up a multiple intelligences classroom

- Research schools that use a multiple intelligences approach by visiting their websites. Try:

  http://www.gardnerschool.org
  http://www.newcityschool.org/home.html
  http://cookps.act.edu.au/mi.htm

  More schools can be found by typing "multiple intelligence school" into a search engine. (Please note that the above websites were in operation at the time of publication.)

- Create intelligence profiles for your class by identifying each student's dominant intelligence(s). This can be done formally or informally.
  Some formal tests can be found on the Internet. Try:

  http://www.mitest.com/omitest.htm
  http://cortland.edu/psych/mi/measure.html
  (will need adapting to a child's level)

  More tests can be found by typing "multiple intelligence checklist" into a search engine. (Please note that the above websites were in operation at the time of publication.)

  Informal methods may include observing work habits, asking students about their interests and hobbies, holding parent–teacher conferences, talking to other teachers, or reading a student's previous school records. A series of checklists to help identify a student's dominant intelligence(s) is also provided on pages x – xi.

- Identify your own dominant intelligence(s) (and, therefore, your teaching approach) by using the checklist on page ix. Use the results to help you decide on the most effective teaching/learning tools for you. You may also like to consider team teaching with other staff members who are dominant in different intelligences. Remember that although you don't have to teach/learn every concept in eight different ways, it is important to develop other teaching styles or intelligences to cater for students who may have different strengths from yours.

- Educate students about multiple intelligences and allow them to discover their own strengths and weaknesses. Discuss how everyone is "wise" in a different way and encourage students to work on their weaknesses. During lessons, show that you value individual differences.

- Allow students to tutor other students using their strong intelligences.

- Encourage students to use their dominant intelligences to aid understanding of topics that would usually require using a weaker intelligence.

- Use a range of methods to assess student work; e.g. traditional tests, role-play, work samples, portfolios. The methods you choose should allow students to demonstrate their intelligence strengths. Some assessment worksheets are found on pages xii – xiii.

Teacher's notes

- Plan cross-curricular units of work that allow students to use all the intelligences. One suggested method of doing this is to brainstorm ideas for each intelligence on a particular topic. For example:

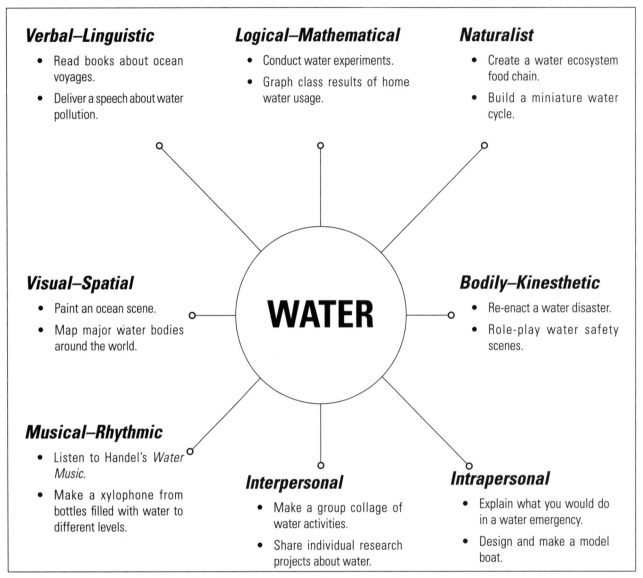

Remember that an activity or task is likely to involve more than one intelligence, but you can choose to focus on a particular intelligence. Another form of planning an overview is illustrated below.

Water							
Verbal–Linguistic	Logical–Mathematical	Naturalist	Visual–Spatial	Bodily–Kinesthetic	Musical–Rhythmic	Interpersonal	Intrapersonal
Read books about ocean voyages. Deliver a speech about water pollution.	Conduct water experiments. Graph class results of home water usage.	Create a water ecosystem food chain. Build a miniature water cycle.	Paint an ocean scene. Map major water bodies around the world.	Re-enact a water disaster. Role-play water safety scenes.	Listen to Handel's *Water Music*. Make a xylophone from bottles filled with water to different levels.	Make a group collage of water activities. Share individual research projects about water.	Explain what you would do in a water emergency. Design and make a model boat.

How to use this book

This book contains six units of work, each of which covers a single topic.
The topics are:

| Space | Water | Life cycles | Festivals | Good health | Dinosaurs |

Each unit consists of the following pages:

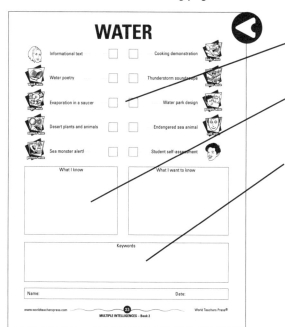

The first page of each unit is a **cover page** designed for the students. It can be glued into student workbooks at the beginning of the unit. Students can fill in the tick boxes to indicate which worksheets and subsequent intelligences have been completed.

Before the students begin work on the unit, they should complete these sections individually. Teachers may ask students to brainstorm possible answers as a class or in small groups first.

A keyword section is provided for students to list words or phrases important to the subject. Students may begin by writing a few and adding to the list as they work through the unit. The words or phrases can be typed directly into the students' preferred Internet search engine to promote the most appropriate response to the topic.

An **overview** for teachers has been included for each unit to provide ideas for activities that focus on each intelligence. You could use these activities to further develop the unit topic with the class or as extension work for more able students.

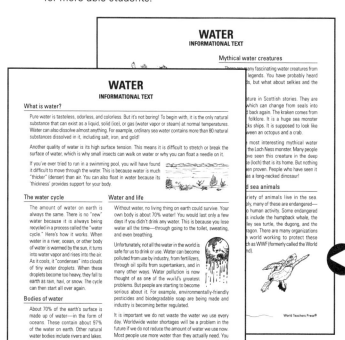

Two pages of general **informational text** about the topic have been provided, written at a student's level of understanding. This text could be used in variety of ways. For example:

- to provide information the students can use in the worksheets,
- for comprehension exercises,
- as a springboard for research projects,
- as a stimulus for class or group discussions.

How to use this book

Eight worksheets are contained in each unit. Each worksheet has been designed to focus on a single intelligence. However, as Gardner has pointed out, every activity we do requires the use of more than one intelligence. Therefore, you will be able to identify other intelligences operating as the students complete the worksheets.

It is advisable that you use each worksheet in the unit to ensure that all the intelligences have been covered.

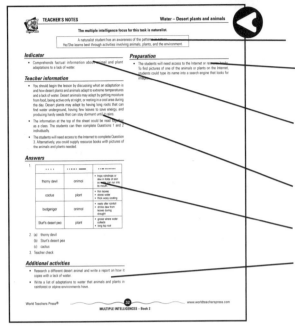

Each worksheet has an accompanying teacher's page.

General information about the dominant intelligence is provided.

Preparation details what needs to be done before the you introduce the activity page to the students. Some materials and preparations are required, others are suggestions.

One or more **indicators** are given for each activity page, providing you with the focus for the activity and the behaviors the students should be demonstrating by completing the activity.

Teacher information provides any information needed to use the worksheet most effectively. It may include background information or suggestions on how to organize the lesson.

Answers, if required, are included.

Additional activities are suggested to further develop the skills and/or concepts taught during the activity. Some of the additional activities will focus on a different intelligence from that of the worksheet—if so, this is indicated.

The **task** and **multiple intelligence** for each worksheet are provided at the top of the page for the student's information.

The **activities** have been selected to focus on the multiple intelligence indicated and cover a range of curriculum areas.

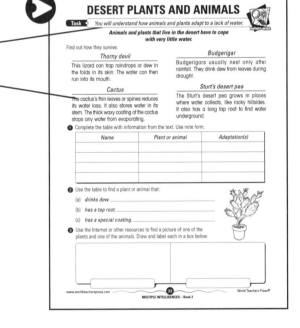

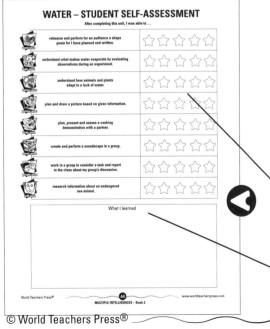

A **student assessment** page completes each unit. It should be given to the students when all the worksheets have been finished.

The students assess their work on the unit by coloring in the stars (with five stars being the best).

What I learned can be completed after the students have brainstormed ideas in small groups or after a class discussion.

© World Teachers Press® www.worldteacherspress.com

Teacher self-assessment worksheet

Find out the intelligences in which you are strongest by checking any statements that are true for you.

Verbal–Linguistic
I like to read during my leisure time. ☐
I enjoy teaching creative writing. ☐
I have strong verbal communication skills. ☐
I am skilled at teaching reading skills. ☐

Logical–Mathematical
I enjoy questioning how things work. ☐
I am an organized, logical person. ☐
I enjoy teaching number skills. ☐
I enjoy problem-solving activities. ☐

Naturalist
I enjoy caring for animals. ☐
I enjoy gardening. ☐
I am interested in environmental issues. ☐
I like teaching science lessons involving nature or natural forces. ☐

Visual–Spatial
I enjoy teaching arts and crafts. ☐
I am skilled in making or building things. ☐
I can easily picture creative ideas in my head. ☐
I am skilled at drawing or painting. ☐

Bodily–Kinesthetic
I enjoy teaching physical education. ☐
I am skilled at dancing or acting. ☐
I enjoy activities that require fine or gross motor skills. ☐
I regularly play a sport for enjoyment. ☐

Musical–Rhythmic
I play a musical instrument or sing well. ☐
I regularly use music and rhythms in the classroom. ☐
I can successfully teach students musical concepts. ☐
I enjoy listening to music. ☐

Interpersonal
I have a wide circle of friends. ☐
I am skilled at teaching students how to develop good relationships with others. ☐
I am a natural leader. ☐
I enjoy working in a group or team. ☐

Intrapersonal
I regularly set and achieve personal goals. ☐
I like teaching lessons about feelings and emotions. ☐
I usually enjoy the time I spend alone. ☐
I have strong beliefs and opinions. ☐

Which intelligences did you score the most checkmarks in? _____
Use these results to reflect on how you teach and how you might change your teaching style to incorporate all of the intelligences.

Assessment of student learning styles worksheet–1

Highlight any statements that describe the student's behaviors or skills.
Write any other appropriate behaviors or skills you have observed.

Student name:

Verbal–Linguistic

The student:

- achieves outstanding results in English.
- enjoys writing stories or poems.
- has an excellent vocabulary.
- enjoys reading.
- is skilled at word games.
- enjoys being read to.
- is skilled at verbal communication.

Other:

Naturalist

The student:

- likes to talk about his/her pets.
- enjoys natural science lessons.
- is fascinated with plants.
- brings natural objects to class to talk about.
- enjoys learning about animals.
- enjoys learning about the environment.

Other:

Logical–Mathematical

The student:

- has excellent number skills.
- enjoys logic puzzles and games.
- often questions how things work.
- is a competent problem-solver.
- enjoys science experiments.
- likes playing board games.
- can organize objects into logical groups.

Other:

Visual–Spatial

The student:

- enjoys arts and crafts lessons.
- interprets visual texts more easily than words.
- is a daydreamer.
- is skilled at making models.
- often doodles on work.
- enjoys viewing movies or pictures.
- enjoys completing visual puzzles like mazes.

Other:

© World Teachers Press®

MULTIPLE INTELLIGENCES – Book 2

www.worldteacherspress.com

Assessment of student learning styles worksheet–2

Highlight any statements that describe the student's behaviors or skills.
Write any other appropriate behaviors or skills you have observed.

Student name:

Bodily–Kinesthetic

The student:

- enjoys physical education lessons.
- has excellent coordination skills.
- has a talent for acting.
- is skilled at craft activities.
- enjoys hands-on activities.
- moves or fidgets at his/her desk.
- enjoys taking objects apart and putting them back together.

Other:

Interpersonal

The student:

- is a natural leader.
- prefers to work in groups or teams.
- has a wide circle of friends.
- is empathetic to others.
- belongs to clubs or other groups.
- enjoys helping others.

Other:

Musical–Rhythmic

The student:

- can play a musical instrument.
- enjoys singing or chanting.
- likes listening to music.
- taps feet or fingers when working.
- demonstrates a good sense of rhythm.
- hums to himself/herself.
- creates his/her own songs.

Other:

Intrapersonal

The student:

- enjoys working on his/her own.
- likes to think about his/her feelings.
- shows independent thought or action.
- can easily express his/her feelings or opinions.
- has a good sense of his/her abilities.
- can set and reach personal goals.

Other:

www.worldteacherspress.com

© World Teachers Press®

Student self-assessment of learning styles worksheet–1

What kind of learner are you? Check the sentences that describe you.

Am I word wise?

I love to read books..............................❑

I like writing stories and poems. ....❑

Word puzzles and games are fun. ....❑

I am good at spelling. ....❑

I enjoy telling news...............................❑

I like learning new words. ....❑

Am I body wise?

I like playing sports.................................❑

I find it hard to sit still at my desk. ....❑

Drama is lots of fun. ....❑

I like to know what objects feel like............❑

I like making things with my hands. ....❑

I prefer to "do" rather than watch..............❑

Am I logic wise?

I like to know how things work....................❑

I love board games like chess....................❑

I enjoy science experiments. ....❑

I like puzzles that make me think................❑

I like trying to solve problems....................❑

Number games are fun. ....❑

Am I picture wise?

Art is my favorite subject...........................❑

I like to do jigsaw puzzles.........................❑

I am good at drawing...............................❑

I can read maps easily. ....❑

I enjoy making models.............................❑

I often have vivid dreams..........................❑

Am I nature wise?

I have a collection of shells, rocks, or other natural objects.................❑

I like to care for animals. ....❑

I enjoy gardening. ....❑

I love to visit museums or zoos...❑

I prefer to be outdoors rather than indoors. ....❑

Looking after the environment is important to me...........................❑

© World Teachers Press®

www.worldteacherspress.com

Student self-assessment of learning styles worksheet–2

What kind of learner are you? Check the sentences that describe you.

Am I music wise?

I like to sing. .... ❏

I play, or would like to play, a musical instrument. .... ❏

When I work, I often tap my feet or my fingers. .... ❏

I enjoy listening to music. .... ❏

I know lots of songs by heart. .... ❏

I enjoy listening to rhymes/raps. .... ❏

Am I people wise?

I enjoy team sports. .... ❏

I like to work in a group. .... ❏

I like sharing my ideas with others. .... ❏

I have more than three close friends. .... ❏

I find it interesting to meet new people. .... ❏

When people around me are happy it makes me feel happy too. .... ❏

Am I self wise?

I do my best schoolwork on my own. .... ❏

I often think about what I will do when I grow up. .... ❏

Staying home is usually more fun than being in a crowd of people. .... ❏

I have one or two close friends. .... ❏

I like to think about how I feel. .... ❏

I write in a diary in my free time. .... ❏

2 Most of your checkmarks should be in one or two learning styles. Which learning style(s) has/have the most checkmarks? Circle the icon(s).

word wise   logic wise   nature wise   picture wise   body wise   music wise   people wise   self wise

3 Complete these sentences.

(a) I have found I am a _____ learner.

(b) Look at the learning styles which you checked the least. Which of these learning styles would

you most like to work on? _____

www.worldteacherspress.com

© World Teachers Press®

MULTIPLE INTELLIGENCES – Book 2

© World Teachers Press®

MULTIPLE INTELLIGENCES – Book 2

www.worldteacherspress.com

SPACE

Informational text ·············· ☐   ☐ ·············· Fit for space

word wise

Planetary poetry ·············· ☐   ☐ ·············· Space symphony

music wise

logic wise

Planet facts ·············· ☐   ☐ ·············· Alien ship

people wise

nature wise

Stargazing ·············· ☐   ☐ ·············· Space diary

self wise

picture wise

Space travel brochure ········· ☐   ☐ ······ Student self-assessment

What I know	What I want to know

Keywords

Name:	Date:

www.worldteacherspress.com

© World Teachers Press®

SPACE OVERVIEW

Verbal–Linguistic

- Make up an alien language according to specific criteria. Write it, work out how to speak it, then use it in a role-play.
- Write a postcard describing a vacation on another planet.
- Create a character profile for an astronaut or alien.
- Read sayings or proverbs that mention the moon, the sun, or the planets. Make up your own.
- Write a magazine advertisement to entice aliens to visit another planet.
- Write planet-shaped or rocket-shaped poems.
- Read about the latest discoveries about Mars.
- Write a play about landing on your "perfect" planet.
- Read Neil Armstrong's biography.
- Perform a space poem in "choral-speaking" form.
- List some fascinating facts about planets or the stars.
- Research a planet. Design a travel brochure for it.
- Write a story about being "lost in space."
- Research various things in space, such as comets, meteors, stars, etc.
- Make a space dictionary.
- Interview an astronaut who has traveled to the moon.
- Create a space quiz.
- Keep a space travel diary.
- Write space poetry about planets, spacecraft, stars, etc.
- Write a story about being chosen to participate in an historic space flight.
- Select a planet and research to present a fact file to the class.
- Make up an ending to a space story starter.
- Write a report about a character from a space movie.

Logical–Mathematical

- Make a comparison chart of specific stars or planets.
- Use a calculator to compare the distances between planets.
- Discuss the likelihood of other planets having life.
- Complete a scale drawing to show the sizes of two or more planets.
- Plot constellations on a grid.
- Write alien messages in code.
- Construct a time line showing the dates planets were discovered.
- Sort planets according to their physical features.
- Make a balloon rocket, test it, and measure it.
- Order the planets in terms of size.
- Write a space code to talk to friends in space.
- Measure the area of space shapes such as the moon, a rocket, a particular star, etc.
- Compare distances to planets from earth and the time taken to get there.
- Create a "new" constellation using a specified number of stars.
- Locate or list coordinates on a grid of a fictional planet or a moon map.
- Calculate the sizes of planets and compare.

Naturalist

- Design an appropriate home for an imaginary space creature. Create a profile first; for example, 1 m in height, lives mainly in trees, eats berries and fruit, lives alone, likes warm weather.
- Write a list of things earth animals would need to survive on a particular planet.
- Locate and observe pictures on the Internet of stars, planets, and comets.
- Make a model of our solar system.
- Find out about the natural features of the moon, such as craters or seas.
- Describe what life might be like on Mars, given the conditions on the planet.
- Compare the physical features of the earth compared to other known planets.
- Discuss why solar and lunar eclipses occur.
- Create a new planet. Name it and describe it, including information about natural features.
- Investigate the environment of various planets.

Visual–Spatial

- Design a wanted poster for a space creature.
- Make models of planets, display and label.
- Construct 3-D rockets from everyday materials.
- Make a tangram spacecraft.
- Illustrate a picture book about space for a young child.
- Watch footage of the first moon landing and discuss.
- Color the planets correctly, according to photos.
- Create space-themed masks, such as an alien, to use for drama.
- Draw and name a new constellation.
- View pictures from space to recreate a space painting.
- Watch space movies such as *E.T.* or *2001 – A space odyssey* and act out a favorite scene.
- Create an alien from a variety of materials.
- Create a scale model of the planets in the solar system or a particular spacecraft.
- Create a picture representing a view of a planet from a spacecraft.
- Design a postcard and stamps from an imaginary planet. Complete the postcards and display.

© World Teachers Press®   www.worldteacherspress.com

MULTIPLE INTELLIGENCES – Book 2

SPACE OVERVIEW

Musical–Rhythmic

- Listen to "space" music from movies. Use as a stimulus to write or draw.
- Write a Morse code message to send to aliens.
- Compose space music for a movie scene using a synthesizer.
- Invite guest musicians to play "space" music such as Holst's *The Planets*.
- Write a rap about exploring space.
- Use percussion instruments to create "space" or "alien" music.
- Clap out rhythms for space terms.
- Rewrite words to simple tunes such as "Twinkle, Twinkle, Little Star" to create space songs.
- Investigate how sound travels through and around the atmosphere of different planets.
- Use musical instruments to make sounds to match each planet.
- Create movements to match space themes such as *Star Wars* or *War of the Worlds*.

Bodily–Kinesthetic

- Develop a "moon" dance with accompanying music and perform it.
- Create a type of sign language or body language to communicate with visiting aliens.
- Design a fitness program for an astronaut.
- Act out legends from other cultures about the moon or stars.
- Role-play an interview with an alien or an astronaut.
- Make a space board game.
- Visit a planetarium or observatory.
- Walk like an astronaut on the moon.
- Investigate body equipment needed to survive in space, such as a spacesuit, air hose, helmet, and food rations.
- Investigate or design the diet for an astronaut.

Interpersonal

- In a group, imagine you are taking part in a reality television show that will be filmed in space. Consider 10 items you think you will need.
- In a group, consider the following problem: "You are one of a group of scientists. You have been asked to study an alien. What information do you want to find out? What experiments will you conduct? Consider the humane treatment of the alien."
- In a group, create a new ending to a space story.
- In groups, design invitations, decorations, and costumes for a "space" party. Plan the food to be provided as well as the games to be played.
- Hold a debate entitled, "All the money spent on space exploration should be spent on projects on earth."
- In groups, design and make a space game. Play it with a different group of students.
- Complete a group project about a particular planet, system, or space feature.
- In pairs or small groups, create television advertisements to attract aliens to visit earth; or to encourage "earthlings" to visit another planet.

Intrapersonal

- Imagine you are taking part in the first mission to Mars. Describe your feelings.
- Imagine what it is like to float in space. Write a description.
- Write a journal entry titled *My journey to the moon*.
- Complete a research project on the planets of our solar system.
- Complete a learning log of space facts.
- Complete the sentence *My space hero is ...* after conducting research.
- Find out what characteristics people from each sign of the zodiac are supposed to have. Compare yourself to the description of your star sign.
- Make a personal time line to place in a time capsule.

SPACE
INFORMATIONAL TEXT

The solar system

The solar system is the name given to the area of space that contains our sun and the nine planets. The Earth is one of those planets orbiting the sun. "Solar" means anything to do with the sun.

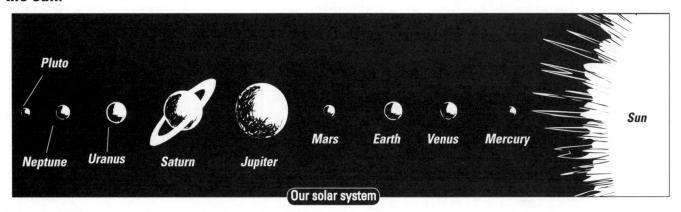

Our solar system

The sun

The star that is the center and the "life" of our solar system is the sun. A huge ball of constantly exploding gas, the sun gives out the heat and light that sustain life on Earth. It has over 700 times the mass of all the planets and their moons put together and has a diameter of 870,000 miles. The sun's enormous gravitational pull keeps its nine satellites and their moons in orbit. Its temperature ranges from 9,900 °F on the surface to 22.5 million °F in the center.

Venus

Venus is only slightly smaller than earth, with a diameter of 7,500 miles. It orbits the sun at a distance of 68 million miles. This planet is covered in smog-like clouds made up of carbon dioxide and sulfuric acid. Although clouds swirl around the planet at great speed and lightning crashes upon it, the surface temperature is about 855 °F. Venus was named after the Roman goddess of love and beauty.

Earth

Earth is the only planet that is thought to contain life forms. Its atmosphere contains water vapour, oxygen, carbon dioxide, and nitrogen. In early times, it was thought that the earth was the center of the universe and that it was flat! With a diameter of 8,000 miles, the earth takes 24 hours to rotate on its axis, giving its inhabitants day and night. Orbiting the sun at a distance of 92 million miles, the temperature of the earth's surface ranges from −128 °F to 136 °F.

Mercury

Mercury is one of the hottest planets, being only 30 million miles away from the sun. Its surface temperature ranges from −300 °F to 800 °F. It is about one-third of the size of the earth, with a diameter of 3,030 miles. Mercury closely resembles our moon, with large craters on its surface. It has no atmosphere and is named after the Roman messenger god.

SPACE
INFORMATIONAL TEXT

Jupiter

Jupiter is the largest planet in our solar system with a diameter of 89,000 miles – 11 times the size of earth! Jupiter has at least 16 moons and a "red-spot" created by liquids and gases, forming clouds and storms. It also has a thin ring that is similar to Saturn's. At 500 million miles from the sun, Jupiter's surface temperature is approximately –100 °F. Its atmosphere consists of methane, ammonium, and some water vapor. Jupiter is named after Jupiter, king of Roman gods, because of its great size.

Pluto

Pluto is the smallest planet in the solar system, being smaller than our moon, with a diameter of 1,430 miles (one quarter of the earth). From Pluto, the sun would look like a little bright star as it is 4 billion miles away. This great distance results in Pluto having a surface temperature of –380 °F and an atmosphere of frozen methane gas. Pluto has one moon named Charon, named after the ferryman who rowed the souls of the dead across the River Styx.

Saturn

Saturn has colored rings that surround it that are made up of ice, dust and rocks. With 23 moons, Saturn has a diameter of 75,000 miles. Although it is 900 million miles from the sun, Saturn can be seen from the earth without a telescope. With a surface temperature of –275 °F, Saturn's atmosphere is similar to Jupiter's, consisting of dense methane and ammonia. The Roman god of harvest and reaping gave his name to this colorful planet.

Neptune

With a surface temperature of –340 °F, it is predicted that life could not exist on this planet. Neptune has two moons and a bluish appearance that may have resulted in the planet being named after the ancient Roman god of the ocean. Scientist believe that Pluto may have been one of Neptune's moons that escaped. Neptune is 2.8 billion miles away from the sun and has an atmosphere of dense methane gas. This planet has a diameter of 31,000 miles.

Uranus

Because Uranus is 1.8 billion miles away from the sun, little is known about it. We do know that it is about four times the size of the earth, with a diameter of 32,000 miles, and that its surface temperature is –330 °F. Uranus has 15 satellites and is a liquid planet with a thick cloudy atmosphere of methane gas. Uranus was named after the ancient Roman god of the heavens.

Mars

Mars, often called the "red planet" due to its blood red appearance, was named after the Roman god of war. With a surface temperature between –200 °F and 32 °F and polar icecaps that melt and freeze with the seasons, Mars is considered to be the planet most similar to the earth. It is about half the size of earth with a diameter of 4,200 miles and orbits at 140 million miles from the sun. The atmosphere on Mars is thin and mainly carbon dioxide. Scientists believe that if the polar icecaps melted, a greenhouse effect would occur that could make it possible for humans to colonize the planet. Mars has two satellites orbiting it.

www.worldteacherspress.com

Teacher's Notes   Space – Planetary poetry

The multiple intelligence focus for this task is verbal–linguistic.

A verbal–linguistic student thinks in words. He/She learns best through activities involving reading, writing, and speaking.

Indicator

- Writes a poem about space.

Teacher information

- Students should have read background information about the planets in the solar system before commencing this task, or have access to information.
- Students should have read or written different forms of poetry before choosing a style of their own to use.

  A **haiku** is a Japanese poem about nature. Each poem is made up of three lines.
  Line ❶ Five syllables and states "where it is"
  Line ❷ Seven syllables and states "what it is" or "what it is doing"
  Line ❸ Five syllables and states "when or what is being felt" or "what is happening"

  A **limerick** is a nonsense poem made up of five lines with a special rhyming pattern.
  Lines ❶ and ❷ rhyme and usually have the same number of syllables.
  Lines ❸ and ❹ rhyme and are shorter than the others.
  Line ❺ rhymes with and usually has the same number of syllables as ❶ and ❷.

  A **cinquain** is a five-line poem that describes something. It does not rhyme and has short sentences.
  Line ❶ Title (one word or two syllables to describe the topic)
  Line ❷ Two words or four syllables to describe the title
  Line ❸ Three words or six syllables to describe what the topic does
  Line ❹ Four words or eight syllables to describe the feeling or mood
  Line ❺ One word or two syllables with a similar meaning to the topic

  A **narrative** poem tells or recites a story.

Preparation

- Look in the resource center for poetry anthology books and borrow some for the classroom.

Answers

1. Teacher check
2. None required
3. Teacher check

Additional activities

- Students present their poems for display.
- Hold a poetry-reading afternoon and allow students to read their poetry to the class.

PLANETARY POETRY

Task — *You will write a poem about space.*

① Write one fact about the sun and each of the planets in the solar system.

Planet	Fact
Sun ☉	
Mercury ☿	
Venus ♀	
Earth ⊕	
Mars ♂	
Jupiter ♃	
Saturn ♄	
Uranus ♅	
Neptune ♆	
Pluto ♇	

② Look through poetry books to find poems about the sky and outer space. Discuss each poem with a partner.

③ Write a poem that describes the night sky. Write your draft below. Your poem can be a haiku, limerick, narrative, cinquain, or in a form of your own choice.

www.worldteacherspress.com

© World Teachers Press®

MULTIPLE INTELLIGENCES – Book 2

TEACHER'S NOTES   Space – Planet facts

The multiple intelligence focus for this task is logical–mathematical.

A logical–mathematical student thinks rationally and in abstractions. He/She learns best through activities involving problem-solving, numbers, and patterns.

Indicator

- Extracts data to complete a table of information about the nine planets in the solar system.

Teacher information

- The solar system contains all the planets, asteroids, and comets that orbit our sun. Early astronomers used their eyes to look at the sky. Today, we use powerful telescopes to view space.

- Looking at the sky, planets look like stars; however, they are much closer to us. Like earth, the other eight planets orbit the sun. Because of this, the planets slowly move across our sky. Venus is the brightest planet and is called the morning star at sunrise; at sunset, it is known as the evening star. The other planet that is visible to the naked eye is Mars.

- The four planets that are the closest to the sun – Mercury, Venus, Earth, and Mars – are made of rock and iron. Jupiter, Saturn, Uranus, and Neptune are balls of gas. Pluto, the ninth planet and the furthest from the sun, is a small frozen ball of gas.

- Discuss charts on display to remember the order of the planets.

- Brainstorm to elicit students' knowledge of the solar system and its planets. Explain that they are going to use the worksheet, books, encyclopedias, and the Internet to discover information about each of the nine planets in the solar system.

- Study the table to be completed. Ensure that the students understand the headings. Talk about one specific planet; for example, Earth.

- Earth – one satellite (the moon); temperature ranges from –128 °F to 136 °F ; nitrogen, oxygen, carbon dioxide, and water vapour form the atmosphere; distance from sun – approx. 92 million miles; diameter – approx. 8,000 miles.

- Students work in pairs or small groups to discover the information about each of the planets.

- Once each group has finished, collate the facts on the board. Were there any discrepancies? Discuss with the class why this might be. Have there been any new discoveries about the planets recently?

Preparation

- On each group of tables, place copies of the worksheet (page 9), books about the solar system, and encyclopedias (letters M, E, V, J, P, S, U, N). Bookmark websites that display information about each of the planets.

- Suggestion: Enlarge the table (page 9) to 11 x 17.

Answers

1. Teacher check with students

Additional activities

- Use the Internet to search for any new discoveries about the planets.

- Paint a solar system onto a black wall. Add the facts about each of the planets to the wall.

- Create a class booklet titled *Amazing planet facts* for students to add to when information is located. Use for interest reading.

PLANET FACTS

Task: You will complete the table of information about the sun and the nine planets in the solar system.

	Satellite(s)	Surface temperature	Distance from sun	Diameter	Atmosphere	Other information
Sun ☉						
Mercury ☿						
Venus ♀						
Earth ⊕						
Mars ♂						
Jupiter ♃						
Saturn ♄						
Uranus ♅						
Neptune ♆						
Pluto ♇						

TEACHER'S NOTES — Space – Stargazing

The multiple intelligence focus for this task is naturalist.

A naturalist student has an awareness of the patterns in nature. He/She learns best through activities involving animals, plants, and the environment.

Indicator

- Observes the night sky and makes inferences about the movement of the stars.
- Describes his/her observations in writing.

Preparation

- Obtain a star map, globe, clear dome-shaped bowl bigger than the globe, small amount of modelling clay or similar.
- Organize a slide projector or video/television to view pictures of the night sky. If it is possible, stick stars (stickers) to the outside of the clear bowl.
- Prior to the lesson, ask the students if a clear night sky is the same whenever they look at it. If they are unsure, they can view the sky on the evenings leading up to the science lesson.

Teacher information

- Discuss the students' observations of the previous nights. What did they see? Was the sky different each night?
- Write the question on the board, "Do the stars move?" Let the students make predictions about the answer.
- Students complete Questions 1 and 2 of the worksheet at home. They return to school and discuss their findings within a small group. Written explanations are completed in Question 3.

  Note: This activity might best be carried out in winter when there are fewer hours of daylight.

- Ask students to volunteer to read their explanation of the previous nights' observations to the class.
- To help students understand this difficult concept, place the globe on a table for the students to view. Stick a blob of clay on the place on the globe representing your location. Hold the bowl over the top of the globe leaving a little distance in between. Explain to the students that the "dome" of stars is around the whole of the earth and the solar systems that it is in. Point to the modeling clay and then slowly turn the Earth. Explain to the class that it is we who moves and that the stars are fixed in our sky. This is why as the Earth rotates for 24 hours on its axis, we see the stars "moving."
- Hold the dome even higher. Ask the students if the stars we see change throughout the year. (They do.) Move the globe around the table to show it traveling on its orbit around the sun. As the earth moves through the year, the stars we see in the sky change.
- As a challenge, students can choose to do further research or write creatively about the stars.

Answers

1. Teacher check
2. Teacher check
3. See background information

Additional activities

- Keep a "stargazing" journal. When looking at the sky each night, students take notes of their thoughts, questions, and comments. Diagrams, extra information, creative writing, and poetry can be written in the journal.
- Research the twelve main star constellations in the zodiac – Aries, Taurus, Gemini, Cancer, Leo, Virgo, Libra, Scorpio, Sagittarius, Capricorn, Aquarius, and Pisces.
- Students sketch the night sky as homework. They recreate the night sky with yellow and white paint on a black background in the classroom.

STARGAZING

Task: *You will observe the night sky, make inferences, and describe your observations in writing.*

① On a clear night, find a spot near your house away from any houselights or street lights.

(a) Look at the night sky. What do you see?

(b) Use four adjectives to describe the sky and how you feel when you look at it.

_____

_____

_____

_____

_____

_____

② Find a place where you can look up at the night sky but also see something stationary, like the top of a roof. Place a rock at your feet so you will be able to return to that spot.

(a) Look at the sky. Choose a cluster of stars. Draw how the stars look in relation to the tip of your stationary object. Take note of the time. Under each picture, draw an arrow showing the direction you are facing. Repeat this procedure twice more at hourly intervals.

(b) Stand in your spot. How high are the cluster of stars you have chosen? Hold out one hand horizontally, thumb up, with your little finger resting on the horizon. Place your other hand on top. Keep doing this until you reach your stars.

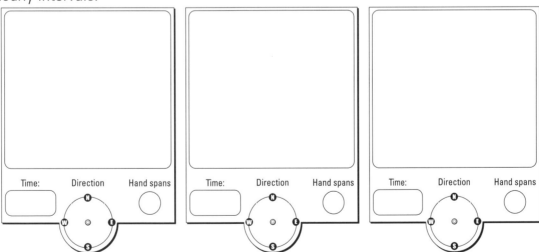

③ Are the stars moving? Explain on a separate sheet of paper why the stars appear to spin across the sky during the night.

TEACHER'S NOTES　　　　　　　　　　　　　Space – Space travel brochure

The multiple intelligence focus for this task is visual–spatial.

> A visual–spatial student thinks in images, colors, and shape.
> He/She learns best through activities involving visualization.

Indicator

- Creates a travel brochure for a chosen planet.

Teacher information

- Show students the travel brochures. Point out the features of each. How effective are they at making the reader want to travel to that place? Individually or in pairs, students choose one planet. They research it further, taking notes about the conditions. Use this information to create a travel brochure for the planet.

Answers

1. Teacher check
2. Teacher check
3. Teacher check

Additional activities

- Compare travel brochures of different planets. View layouts and information included.
- Display travel brochures on a wall titled "Space vacations."
- Write a travel diary entry about a vacation to a particular planet. (verbal-linguistic)

Preparation

- Collect a variety of travel brochures.
- Provide extra equipment needed to produce the brochures, such as art paper and markers.

SPACE TRAVEL BROCHURE

Task — *You will create a travel brochure for a specific planet.*

1. Complete the boxes below to plan your brochure.

    I have chosen _____ *for my brochure.*

    I will include the following facts about the planet:

    ☾ _____
    ☾ _____
    ☾ _____
    ☾ _____
    ☾ _____
    ☾ _____

2. Draft the design for your brochure and label the sections to show presentation details such as color, photographs to be included, and slogans to be used.

3. Use a separate sheet of paper to create your brochure.

TEACHER'S NOTES Space – Fit for space!

The multiple intelligence focus for this task is bodily–kinesthetic.

A bodily-kinesthetic student has good physical awareness.
He/She learns best through "hands-on" activities.

Indicator

- Plans an exercise regime for an astronaut.

Preparation

- Obtain and read accounts of the types of duties an astronaut is expected to perform while in space, as well as any information about the pressure being in space places upon his or her body.
- Discuss different exercises and their impact upon parts of the body. For example, fast running will develop lung capacity and leg strength, while push-ups will develop upper body and arm strength.

Teacher information

- Students should have a knowledge of exercise and diet requirements for basic health and fitness.
- Students may wish to work individually, in pairs, or in small groups to complete this activity.
- For Question 2, students check the exercise(s) they found worked well for them.

Answers

1. Teacher check
2. Teacher check
3. Teacher check
4. Teacher check

Additional activities

- Write an appropriate diet for an astronaut. Discuss the different food groups and the benefits each provides. (visual–linguistic)
- Selected students give a talk about the fitness program they use to enable them to participate in their individual sporting or leisure activities and demonstrate some of their exercises for the class. (bodily–kinesthetic)

FIT FOR SPACE!

Task

You will plan, complete, and record an exercise program suitable for an astronaut.

body wise

1 List some physical skills needed to maintain fitness on a space journey.

2 Write some exercises needed to maintain or develop these skills.

- _____ | I have tried this exercise and it works well! | YES | NO |
- _____ | I have tried this exercise and it works well! | YES | NO |
- _____ | I have tried this exercise and it works well! | YES | NO |
- _____ | I have tried this exercise and it works well! | YES | NO |
- _____ | I have tried this exercise and it works well! | YES | NO |

3 Complete the weekly exercise chart below and indicate the number of times each exercise should be performed.

Monday	Tuesday	Wednesday	Thursday	Friday

4 Carry out the exercise program for one week then, on a separate sheet of paper, evaluate the program and make any changes necessary.

www.worldteacherspress.com

15

© World Teachers Press®

MULTIPLE INTELLIGENCES – Book 2

TEACHER'S NOTES   Space – Space symphony

The multiple intelligence focus for this task is musical–rhythmic.

> A musical–rhythmic student has an awareness of music and sound.
> He/She learns best through activities involving music and rhythms.

Indicator

- Evaluates music used to accompany a movie scene.

Preparation

- Before the lesson, select and record a scene from a movie such as *Star Wars*, *War of the Worlds*, or *2001 – A Space Odyssey* where music has been used to enhance the scene.

Teacher information

- Films, videos, or television programs use music to indicate an exciting or suspenseful segment of the story, different emotions or a particular character.
- Students may wish to view a scene more than once in order to describe the music or sounds effects adequately.
- Allow students to discuss their opinions with others if they are experiencing difficulty.

Answers

- Teacher check

Additional activities

- Students listen to theme songs or music from television programs such as *Alf*, *My Favorite Martian* and movies such as *E.T.*, *Alien*, or *Species* and discuss their appropriateness.
- View a scene from a popular movie without sound and discuss how music and sound contribute to the movie.

SPACE SYMPHONY

Task — *You will evaluate music used in movies.*

❶ View a suspenseful scene in the movie, then briefly describe what happened.

Title of movie

Description of scene

❷ View the scene again, noting the music or sound effects heard.

Music

Sound effects

❸ Use your notes to explain how the music and sound effects contributed to the scene.

_____
_____
_____
_____
_____

❹ List movies, videos, or television shows about space or aliens which depict a character by using a particular musical theme for that character.

TEACHER'S NOTES

Space – Alien ship

The multiple intelligence focus for this task is interpersonal.

> An interpersonal student enjoys being in groups of teams.
> He/She learns best through activities involving working with others.

Indicator

- Designs and makes an alien spaceship.

Preparation

- Find and display pictures of different types of spacecraft cut from newspapers or magazines for student perusal.
- Discuss various features of each spacecraft, making comparisons.

Teacher information

- Many interpersonal intelligence activities may be completed as intrapersonal intelligence activities depending on the skills which need to be reinforced. Interpersonal activities seek to develop skills such as cooperation, discussion, and negotiation, while intrapersonal activities develop skills such as time management, motivation, research skills, and self-evaluation.

Answers

- Teacher check

Additional activities

- Display spacecraft on a wall with a space background created by the students. (visual–spatial)
- Give an evaluation of your design to the class, detailing any improvements which may be needed. (verbal–linguistic)
- Create a space station suitable for sustaining the lives of 100 humans in a multinational space program. (interpersonal)

ALIEN SHIP

Task — *You will design and make an alien ship.*

1. In your group, discuss and decide on a suitable design for your ship. Draw your design and label the parts.

2. Write a list of the equipment you need.

   _____
   _____
   _____
   _____

3. Allocate tasks for each member of the group.

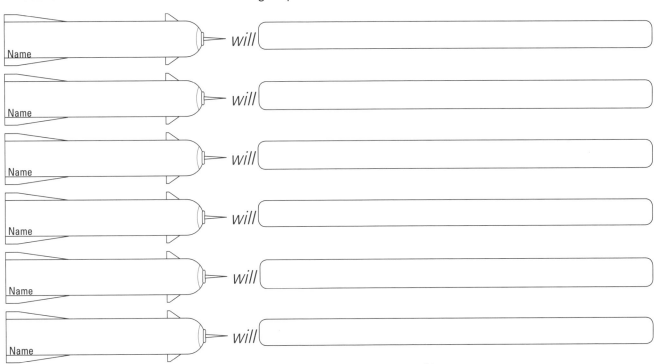

4. Make your design.

5. Evaluate how well you worked as a group.

   "We think …

TEACHER'S NOTES   Space – Space diary

The multiple intelligence focus for this task is intrapersonal.

An intrapersonal student understands and analyzes his/her thoughts and feelings. He/She learns best through individual activities.

Indicator

- Completes and illustrates a diary entry about a space trip.

Teacher information

- Discuss the activity with the students, detailing what is required in each section. Students may suggest different events or answers to complete various sections to motivate other students.

Answers

- Teacher check

Additional activities

- Students write diary entries relevant to other learning areas such as the diary for a scientist making a significant discovery, or a mathematician finally discovering the solution to a specific problem.

Preparation

- Students should be familiar with writing diary entries before commencing this task.
- Read other diaries where a journey is traced over time. These diary excerpts may be those of famous explorers or people who participate in endurance events, for example.

© World Teachers Press®   MULTIPLE INTELLIGENCES – Book 2   www.worldteacherspress.com

SPACE DIARY

Task — You will complete and illustrate a diary entry about a space trip.

1 Complete the diary and illustrate the events of the trip.

Monday _____ (date)

This morning we took off on our adventure into outer space. _____

_____ was in charge and _____

_____

_____

Tuesday _____ (date)

Today we woke up early and _____

_____

_____

_____

_____

Wednesday _____ (date)

Something exciting happened today! We actually saw _____

_____

_____

_____

Thursday _____ (date)

We finally reached _____ this afternoon. I took lots of photos to show _____. Here is my favorite.

Friday _____ (date)

I'm feeling rather tired and _____

_____ doesn't like the rehydrated food.

Saturday _____ (date)

On our way back to Earth, we whizzed past _____

_____

Sunday _____ (date)

Late this afternoon our journey came to an end. We arrived safely back on Earth and _____ was there to meet us. What an amazing experience!

SPACE – STUDENT SELF-ASSESSMENT

After completing this unit, I was able to …

word wise	write a poem about space.	☆ ☆ ☆ ☆ ☆
logic wise	extract data to complete a table of information about the nine planets in our solar system.	☆ ☆ ☆ ☆ ☆
nature wise	observe the night sky and make inferences about the movement of the stars in the night sky.	☆ ☆ ☆ ☆ ☆
picture wise	create a travel brochure for a chosen planet.	☆ ☆ ☆ ☆ ☆
body wise	plan an exercise regime for an astronaut.	☆ ☆ ☆ ☆ ☆
music wise	evaluate music used to accompany a movie scene.	☆ ☆ ☆ ☆ ☆
people wise	design and make an alien spaceship.	☆ ☆ ☆ ☆ ☆
self wise	complete and illustrate a diary entry about a space trip.	☆ ☆ ☆ ☆ ☆

What I learned

© World Teachers Press®   www.worldteacherspress.com

WATER

Informational text ⬚   ⬚ Cooking demonstration

word wise

Water poetry ⬚   ⬚ Thunderstorm soundscape

music wise

logic wise

Evaporation in a saucer ⬚   ⬚ Water park design

people wise

nature wise

Desert plants and animals ⬚   ⬚ Endangered sea animal

self wise

picture wise

Sea monster alert! ⬚   ⬚ Student self-assessment

What I know	What I want to know

Keywords

Name:	Date:

www.worldteacherspress.com   23   © World Teachers Press®

MULTIPLE INTELLIGENCES – Book 2

WATER OVERVIEW

Verbal–Linguistic

- Read books about ocean voyages and write reviews.
- Deliver a speech about water pollution.
- Write a playscript set on the *Titanic*.
- Perform a radio play that uses some water sound effects.
- Invite a guest speaker to talk to the class about his or her "water" occupation; e.g. marine biologist, diver.
- Write descriptive words about rain.
- Create a poster about water safety.
- Explain how to perform a swimming stroke.
- Write a list of amazing water facts.
- Investigate water conservation measures.
- Write a poem that describes the ocean.
- Write a report on a water animal or plant.
- Create a poster for using water wisely.

Naturalist

- Find out which features water mammals have in common.
- Conduct a scavenger hunt at a beach. Use the collected objects to make collages or sculptures.
- Experiment with watering a plant to find out the correct amount of water it needs.
- Find out the effect water pollution has on plants and animals.
- Create a food chain from a water ecosystem.
- Discuss some environmental water problems such as salinity or drought.
- Compare freshwater and saltwater animals and plants.
- Use the Internet to find out more about environmental organizations.
- Research and build a miniature water cycle.
- Research the importance of water to animals and people.

Logical–Mathematical

- Conduct experiments concerning the different states of water – solid, liquid, gas.
- Graph class results of water usage at home and discuss any patterns or trends found.
- Predict the outcome of swimming races, given the athletes' statistics.
- Predict the probability of rainfall on a particular day of the year.
- Complete logic puzzles or brainteasers that have a water theme.
- Perform experiments that compare fresh water to salt water.
- Design the "perfect" water animal, based on observations of real animals.
- Calculate the daily cost of water consumption in your home.

- Find out how long ice takes to melt under different conditions.
- Calculate how long it would take for a puddle to dry up.
- Categorize lists of water facts and explain the groupings chosen.
- Study the percentage of water in the total body weight for different animals and plants.
- Investigate what percentage of people in the world do not have access to clean drinking water.
- Explore floating and sinking after making predictions.
- Use a variety of containers to investigate liquid measures using water.
- Investigate and measure water displacement.

Visual–Spatial

- Visualize how water moves in different situations and perform a group movement piece.
- Make modeling clay models of water creatures.
- Analyze a water painting or photo.
- Paint an ocean scene. Design a travel brochure that uses inviting images of the sea.
- Make paper-mâché models of deep-sea animals.
- Using everyday materials, design a boat that will float.
- Collect shells at the beach and make a necklace from them.

- Create a collage using pictures of water found in magazines. Include freshwater and saltwater scenes, drinks, sprinklers, water recreational activities, etc.
- Look through surfing magazines to find a photograph of a surfer riding a large wave. Cut the picture in half lengthways and glue it to a sheet of paper. Students can complete the picture using their choice of materials; e.g. colored pencils, crayons, paint, etc.
- Map major water bodies around the world.
- Blow bubbles and investigate their size.

© World Teachers Press®   www.worldteacherspress.com

WATER OVERVIEW

Bodily–Kinesthetic

- Conduct an excursion to a dam.
- Mime drinking a glass of water, having a shower, washing the car, etc.
- Perform a play about imaginary water creatures; e.g. mermaids, the Loch Ness Monster, etc.
- Learn how different animals move through the water.
- In a small group, re-enact a water disaster.
- Learn some of the hand signals divers use.
- Role-play water safety scenes.
- Make a model of a device for making salt water drinkable.
- Set up and investigate a class aquarium.
- Make an aquatic diorama.

Musical–Rhythmic

- Listen to Handel's *Water Music* and describe how it makes you feel.
- Make a xylophone using bottles filled with water to varying levels.
- Listen to whale and dolphin sounds on CD while working in class.
- Create "water sounding" music using percussion instruments.
- Create movements to match water-themed music such as sea shanties, pieces of classical music, or relaxation CDs with water as a feature.
- Find or create suitable music to devise an underwater dance.
- Write a song about the ocean and perform it with musical instruments.

Interpersonal

- Discuss different environmental "water" issues and what can be done.
- Choose an endangered water animal. In a group, devise an action plan to help it.
- Discuss what would need to change in your life if you wanted to train for an Olympic Games swimming team.
- Share individual research projects about water with a partner or small group.
- Prepare a one-minute television commercial in a small group to promote the health benefits of drinking six to eight glasses of water a day.
- In a small group, devise an experiment that tests water properties. Demonstrate it for the class.
- In a group, design and make a waterwheel.
- In a group, create a water toy.
- Make a group collage that depicts various water activities.

Intrapersonal

- Describe a "water" career you would most like to have; e.g. dolphin trainer, swimmer.
- Write what you would do in given water emergencies.
- Describe how a stormy sea, a calm lake, or a flowing river makes you feel.
- Write your feelings about water pollution.
- Consider which water sports you would most like to try.
- Select a "water" topic such as water pollution or the sea and complete an individual research project.
- Research and construct a time line to show the history of water transportation.
- Keep a diary to show how much water you use over a week.
- Design and make a model boat.

www.worldteacherspress.com   © World Teachers Press®

WATER
INFORMATIONAL TEXT

What is water?

Pure water is tasteless, odorless, and colorless. But it's not boring! To begin with, it is the only natural substance that can exist as a liquid, solid (ice), or gas (water vapor or steam) at normal temperatures. Water can also dissolve almost anything. For example, ordinary sea water contains more than 80 natural substances dissolved in it, including salt, iron, and gold!

Another quality of water is its high surface tension. This means it is difficult to stretch or break the surface of water, which is why small insects can walk on water or why you can float a needle on it.

If you've ever tried to run in a swimming pool, you will have found it difficult to move through the water. This is because water is much "thicker" (denser) than air. You can also float in water because its "thickness" provides support for your body.

The water cycle

The amount of water on earth is always the same. There is no "new" water because it is always being recycled in a process called the "water cycle." Here's how it works. When water in a river, ocean, or other body of water is warmed by the sun, it turns into water vapor and rises into the air. As it cools, it "condenses" into clouds of tiny water droplets. When these droplets become too heavy, they fall to earth as rain, hail, or snow. The cycle can then start all over again.

Bodies of water

About 70% of the earth's surface is made up of water—in the form of oceans. These contain about 97% of the water on earth. Other natural water bodies include rivers and lakes. There are also artificially created water bodies, such as reservoirs and canals.

Water and life

Without water, no living thing on earth could survive. Your own body is about 70% water! You would last only a few days if you didn't drink any water. This is because you lose water all the time—through going to the toilet, sweating, and even breathing.

Unfortunately, not all the water in the world is safe for us to drink or use. Water can become polluted from use by industry, from fertilizers, through oil spills from supertankers, and in many other ways. Water pollution is now thought of as one of the world's greatest problems. But people are starting to become serious about it. For example, environmentally-friendly pesticides and biodegradable soap are being made and industry is becoming better regulated.

It is important we do not waste the water we use every day. Worldwide water shortages will be a problem in the future if we do not reduce the amount of water we use now. Most people use more water than they actually need. You can help save water by taking shorter showers, turning off the tap when you brush your teeth and washing dishes in the sink.

WATER
INFORMATIONAL TEXT

Water activities

We don't only need to water to survive—we can also use it for fun! Some water activities are fast, like jet skiing and whitewater rafting. Others don't cause any noise or pollution, such as canoeing and swimming. Some people enjoy exploring underwater by snorkeling and diving.

One water activity many people enjoy is visiting a water park. These have a variety of waterslides and rides which can be fun—or terrifying!

Adaptations to water

Some animals have had to adapt to a lack of water in their environments. Animals and plants living in desert regions have some particularly amazing adaptations. For example, a camel can drink up to 60 gallons of water at one time and can also survive without drinking again for up to a week! The Sturt's desert pea, like many other desert plants, has a very long tap root to help it find water underground.

Mythical water creatures

There are many fascinating water creatures from myths and legends. You have probably heard of mermaids, but what about selkies and the kraken?

Selkies feature in Scottish stories. They are creatures which can change from seals into humans and back again. The kraken comes from Norwegian folklore. It is a huge sea monster which attacks ships. It is supposed to look like a cross between an octopus and a crab.

One of the most interesting mythical water creatures is the Loch Ness monster. Many people claim to have seen this creature in the deep Scottish lake (loch) that is its home. But nothing has ever been proven. People who have seen it describe it as a long-necked dinosaur!

Endangered sea animals

A huge variety of animals live in the sea. Unfortunately, many of these are endangered—often due to human activity. Some endangered sea animals include the humpback whale, the Kemp's Ridley sea turtle, the dugong, and the leafy sea dragon. There are many organizations around the world working to protect these animals, such as WWF (formerly called the World Wildlife Fund).

TEACHER'S NOTES

Water – Watery poetry

The multiple intelligence focus for this task is verbal–linguistic.

A verbal–linguistic student thinks in words.
He/She learns best through activities involving reading, writing, and speaking.

Indicators

- Plans and writes a shape poem with a water theme.
- Rehearses and performs a poem for an audience.

Teacher information

- Shape (or concrete) poems look like the topic being written about. The lines are written around or inside the outline of the subject. The size of the words can change to reflect the meaning.
- Before the students complete the worksheet, you could show copies of a range of shape poems. The students can then complete Question 1.
- If the students are having problems brainstorming words for Question 2, you could ask the class to help write on the board a list of words for each topic given.
- Advise students to write their poems in pencil first when completing Question 4.
- Before students begin practicing their poems, you should read aloud some of the shape poems brought for the lesson, varying pitch, pace, pausing, and volume to demonstrate how vocal expression can enhance meaning. You should discuss how your voice changed for a word or line and give reasons why.
- The students can present their poems to a small group or the whole class. If some students are uncomfortable about doing this, they could practice and present their poems with a partner.

Answers

- Teacher check

Additional activities

- Write poems with a water theme in other forms; e.g. sonnets, haiku, limericks.
- Perform published poems with a water theme as group movement pieces. (bodily-kinesthetic)

Preparation

- Each student will need scrap paper to write the draft of his/her poem.
- Collect examples of shape poems to share with students.

© World Teachers Press® www.worldteacherspress.com

MULTIPLE INTELLIGENCES – Book 2

WATERY POETRY

Task — You will rehearse and perform for an audience a shape poem you have planned and written.

A "shape" poem is written in the shape of the object it is about.

For example:

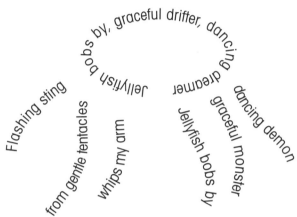

① Try your own water shape poem. Circle one of the topics below or choose your own.

waterfall   waterslide   wave
shark   eel   seaweed

② Brainstorm a list of words that describe your topic's movement, colors, sounds, shapes, or feel. Check your favorites.

③ Use the words you checked to help you write your poem on a piece of scrap paper. Your poem should be between 8 and 12 lines long.

④ Use a pencil to lightly sketch in the box below the shape your poem is going to be. Write your poem to fit the shape.

⑤ Practice reading your poem aloud, thinking about how you can change the volume, speed, or pitch of each word to make it sound interesting.

Write some notes about this below.

⑥ Read your poem aloud to the class or a small group.

TEACHER'S NOTES   **Water – Evaporation in a saucer**

The multiple intelligence focus for this task is logical–mathematical.

> A logical–mathematical student thinks rationally and in abstractions.
> He/She learns best through activities involving problem-solving, numbers, and patterns.

Indicators

- Predicts the results of an experiment.
- Records observations during an experiment.
- Identifies the conditions that cause water to evaporate.

Preparation

- Organize the students into groups of three or four.
- Each group of students will require three saucers (labeled with their group members' names), a measuring jug, and a jug of water.
- Three areas will need to be set up for the experiment: an area in the sun; a large table away from any windows; and a dark, cool cupboard.
- A timer could sit at the front of the classroom to alert the groups to the correct times to check their saucers. One or two groups at a time could check their saucers.

Teacher information

- You should read the information at the top of the worksheet to the class before the students begin the experiment. The students can then set up their saucers and place them in the three areas. They can then answer Question 3 individually.
- Allow the groups of students to check their saucers at the end of each hour and write their observations in the table.
- Students could discuss the answers to Questions 5 and 6 in their groups before they complete them individually.
- Hold a class discussion about the experiment after the students have completed Questions 5 and 6. The concept that evaporation takes place when water is heated should be the focus. The teacher may like to remind students that they will have seen water turn into gas if they have watched water boiling on a stove.

Answers

- Answers will vary, but should indicate that the water in the saucer left in the sun has evaporated because it has been heated. The amount of water left in the other saucers will vary, depending on the warmth of the room.

Additional activities

- Conduct experiments that demonstrate other qualities of water like condensation and surface tension.
- Make mini-water cycles in jars by filling the jar with a layer of rocks and soil and planting a plant. A bottle cap filled with water should be added before jar is sealed and put in a sunny place.

© World Teachers Press®   www.worldteacherspress.com

MULTIPLE INTELLIGENCES – Book 2

EVAPORATION IN A SAUCER

Task — *You will understand what makes water evaporate by evaluating operations during an experiment.*

Water can exist as a liquid, a solid (ice), or a gas (water vapor or steam). Water changes into a gas through a process called "evaporation." Try this experiment on a sunny afternoon to find out how evaporation occurs.

You will need:
three saucers
a jug of water
a measuring jug
a pencil

① Pour the same amount of water on each saucer. It should be just enough to cover the bottom.

② Place each saucer in one of these places:

saucer ❶   outside the classroom in the sun
saucer ❷   on a table inside
saucer ❸   inside a cupboard

③ What do you think will happen to the water by the end of the afternoon?

saucer ❶ _____

saucer ❷ _____

saucer ❸ _____

④ Complete the table every hour for three hours to explain what happens to the water.

	End of hour 1	End of hour 2	End of hour 3
Saucer 1			
Saucer 2			
Saucer 3			

⑤ What happened? _____

_____

_____

⑥ Why do you think it happened? _____

_____

_____

www.worldteacherspress.com   © World Teachers Press®

MULTIPLE INTELLIGENCES – Book 2

Teacher's Notes

Water – Desert plants and animals

The multiple intelligence focus for this task is naturalist.

A naturalist student has an awareness of the patterns in nature.
He/She learns best through activities involving animals, plants, and the environment.

Indicator

- Comprehends factual information about animal and plant adaptations to a lack of water.

Teacher information

- You should begin the lesson by discussing what an adaptation is and how desert plants and animals adapt to extreme temperatures and a lack of water. Desert animals may adapt by getting moisture from food, being active only at night, or resting in a cool area during the day. Desert plants may adapt by having long roots that can find water underground, having few leaves to save energy, and producing hardy seeds that can stay dormant until it rains.

- The information at the top of the sheet could be read together as a class. The students can then complete Questions 1 and 2 individually.

- The students will need access to the Internet to complete Question 3. Alternatively, you could supply resource books with pictures of the animals and plants needed.

Preparation

- The students will need access to the Internet or resource books. To find pictures of one of the animals or plants on the Internet, students could type its name into a search engine that looks for images.

Answers

1.

Name	Plant or animal?	Adaptation(s)
thorny devil	animal	• traps raindrops or dew in folds of skin so water can run into its mouth.
cactus	plant	• thin leaves • stores water • thick waxy coating
budgerigar	animal	• nests after rainfall • drinks dew from leaves during drought
Sturt's desert pea	plant	• grows where water collects • long tap root

2. (a) thorny devil
   (b) Sturt's desert pea
   (c) cactus
3. Teacher check

Additional activities

- Research a different desert animal and write a report on how it copes with a lack of water.
- Write a list of adaptations to water that animals and plants in rainforest or alpine environments have.

DESERT PLANTS AND ANIMALS

Task — You will understand how animals and plants adapt to a lack of water.

Animals and plants that live in the desert have to cope with very little water.

Find out how they survive.

Thorny devil
This lizard can trap raindrops or dew in the folds in its skin. The water can then run into its mouth.

Cactus
The cactus's thin leaves or spines reduces its water loss. It also stores water in its stem. The thick waxy coating of the cactus stops any water from evaporating.

Budgerigar
Budgerigars usually nest only after rainfall. They drink dew from leaves during drought.

Sturt's desert pea
The Sturt's desert pea grows in places where water collects, like rocky hillsides. It also has a long tap root to find water underground.

1 Complete the table with information from the text. Use note form.

Name	Plant or animal	Adaptation(s)

2 Use the table to find a plant or animal that:

(a) *drinks dew.* _____

(b) *has a tap root.* _____

(c) *has a special coating.* _____

3 Use the Internet or other resources to find a picture of one of the plants and one of the animals. Draw and label each in a box below.

TEACHER'S NOTES

Water – Sea monster alert!

The multiple intelligence focus for this task is visual–spatial.

> A visual–spatial student thinks in images, colors, and shape.
> He/She learns best through activities involving visualization.

Indicator

- Plans and draws a picture based on given information.

Preparation

- The students will require drawing materials such as crayons or pencils.

Teacher information

- You may like to discuss "eyewitness" accounts of creatures like the Loch Ness monster before the students complete the worksheet. Information on the Loch Ness monster can be found at these websites: <http://www.loch-ness.org/> and <http://www.lochness.co.uk/>.
- The students should complete the worksheet individually. Depending on the students' ability, some ideas for Question 2 could be brainstormed as a class.
- Ask the students to share their sea monster pictures with the class. Discuss the differences and why they might have occurred.

Answers

- Answers will vary

Additional activities

- Write a story about the sea monster you created.
  (verbal–linguistic)
- In a small group, design a range of sea monster souvenirs.
  (interpersonal)
- Enlarge your sea monster drawing to poster size. Add some information about sightings of your monster that you think would appeal to tourists.

SEA MONSTER ALERT!

Task — *You will plan and draw a picture based on given information.*

Imagine you are an artist living in a seaside town. Recently, some people have claimed they have seen a huge sea monster close to shore. Here are four people's descriptions.

long neck, big flippers, horns, fat, green, scaly body	dragon-like head, elephant's trunk, short neck, dark green back, pale green belly
big flippers with claws, pointed tail, six legs, skinny, scaly body	stubby tail, two horns on its head, four legs

The mayor of the town wants to use the sea monster story to attract tourists to the town. He asks you to draw a picture of the monster based on the descriptions above. The picture will be used in posters and on souvenirs.

You notice right away that some of the descriptions do not match, but the mayor doesn't seem to care. He asks you to do your best.

❶ Circle the body parts you will use for your drawing.

❷ Write notes about the following before you start drawing.

The colors you will use.

The texture of monster's skin (how it would feel) and how you will create this.

How does the monster move through the water?

❸ Draw a picture of the sea monster in the space below.

TEACHER'S NOTES

Water – Cooking demonstration

The multiple intelligence focus for this task is bodily–kinesthetic.

> A bodily–kinesthetic student has good physical awareness.
> He/She learns best through "hands-on" activities.

Indicators

- Plans and presents a cooking demonstration with a partner.
- Self-assesses a demonstration presented with a partner.

Teacher information

- You may like to ask a cafeteria staff member or a parent to demonstrate a recipe to the class before the worksheet is given to the students. The important features of a demonstration could then be discussed; e.g. clear steps, precise movements, expressive voice.
- Allow the students a set amount of time to find an appropriate recipe. Alternatively, you could find appropriate recipes and give each pair one of them to demonstrate.
- Allow the students time to plan and rehearse their demonstrations.
- After all the demonstrations have been presented, each student should complete Question 5. The answers could then be discussed, focusing on what makes a demonstration successful.

Answers

- Teacher check

Additional activities

- Pairs of students could demonstrate a water experiment to the class.
- Demonstrate a water recipe using mime. The class has to guess what is being mimed.

Preparation

- Collect appropriate cooking equipment and ingredients. You may like to ask students to bring relevant items for their recipes from home.
- Students will need access to Internet recipe websites (e.g. <http://www.allrecipes.com/> or simply type "water recipes" into a search engine) or recipe books to find appropriate recipes to demonstrate.
- Organize the students into pairs.
- A large area that can be easily cleaned, will be required for the rehearsals and the presentations.
- A large table will be required for the students to use during their demonstrations.

COOKING DEMONSTRATION

Task: You will plan, present, and assess a cooking demonstration with a partner.

❶ With a partner, find a simple recipe you could demonstrate to the class.
The recipe:
- *must contain water in some form (e.g. tap water, ice, mineral water, soda water);*
- *should be able to be broken into six steps or fewer.*

❷ Plan your demonstration in the space below.

What are you going to make?
What ingredients and equipment will you need?
What do you need to prepare before the demonstration?
Write the steps you will need to show the class.
❶
❷
❸
❹
❺
❻

❸ Rehearse your demonstration with your partner.
Remember to take turns to speak or demonstrate things.

❹ Present your demonstration to the class.

❺ Answer these questions after your presentation.

(a) What were the best things about your demonstration? _____

_____

(b) How could it have been improved? _____

TEACHER'S NOTES

Water – Thunderstorm soundscape

The multiple intelligence focus for this task is musical–rhythmic.

> A musical–rhythmic student has an awareness of music and sound.
> He/She learns best through activities involving music and rhythms.

Indicator

- In a group, creates and performs a "soundscape."

Teacher information

- Hold a discussion about what sounds might be heard during a thunderstorm. A thunderstorm sound effects CD could be played before or after the discussion.

- You should use the gathered materials to make some thunderstorm noises and ask students for their opinions. The students could suggest what other objects might make appropriate noises. Some could volunteer vocal sound effects.

- You may like to allow the students to bring in their own noise-making materials from home, once they have discussed the soundscape in their groups.

- A time limit for the group discussion and rehearsal of the soundscape should be set. It is suggested that two or three 20-minute sessions should be given. As the rehearsals will be noisy, the groups will need to be separate from each other.

- Once the students feel they are ready, each group should perform its soundscape to the class or record it for playing back later.

- A discussion of the presentations should follow, where the class can give their opinions of how easy the soundscapes were to follow and what objects made the most effective noises.

Answers

- Teacher check

Additional activities

- Write a script for a soundscape, giving directions on the sequence of sound effects and for how long each should be performed.

- Use some of the more effective soundscapes or 'thunderstorm' music as a stimulus for creative writing.

Preparation

- Collect a range of materials that could be used to make thunderstorm sound effects; for example, cardboard, drums, shakers, paper, water in jugs, trays, buckets.

- A thunderstorm sound effects CD may be useful for students to listen to before they begin to prepare their soundscapes.

- Organize the students into groups of four.

- A tape recorder will be required if you wish the students to record their presentations.

THUNDERSTORM SOUNDSCAPE

Task *You will create and perform a "soundscape" in a group.*

Find a group of four people to create a thunderstorm "soundscape." A soundscape is a story told through sound. The story you will tell is of someone walking out on a balcony to sit down and watch a thunderstorm.

❶ Write how you could make each of these sounds. Consider objects and/or voices.

person opening door	
person walking	
person sitting down	
thunder	
light rain	
heavy rain	
wind howling	
objects falling over or breaking	

❷ Write which member(s) of your group will be in charge of each sound effect. You can also write more notes for each part of the story if you need to. Practice your soundscape.

Story	*Who*
Beginning *person opens door, walks out, and sits down*	
Middle *storm begins*	
storm builds up	
storm at its worst	
End *storm dies down, person returns inside*	

❸ Present your soundscape to the class. You could either record it or perform it live! The audience members should close their eyes when they are listening.

www.worldteacherspress.com

MULTIPLE INTELLIGENCES – Book 2

© World Teachers Press®

TEACHER'S NOTES

Water – Water park design

The multiple intelligence focus for this task is interpersonal.

An interpersonal student enjoys being in groups or teams.
He/She learns best through activities involving working with others.

Indicators

- Works in a group to consider an open-ended task.
- Reports to peers about group discussions.

Teacher information

- Read through the entire worksheet with the class. Ask the students for examples of good reasons for the locations and design of each item; e.g. "The toddler pool could be built under the trees so there is some shade. The pool should be shallow so it is safe."
- Before the groups begin work, emphasize that this is an open-ended task; i.e. there are no right or wrong answers. They may also use existing features for any of the items required; e.g. use a hill to create a slope for one of the water slides.
- Each student should draw on his/her map as the group makes decisions.
- Set a time limit for the groups to complete the worksheet. This will vary according to the ability of the class. When the groups have finished their designs, they should divide the explanation of their design among the four group members, taking it in turns to explain various features of their map.

Answers

- Teacher check

Additional activities

- Give groups of students other open-ended tasks associated with water to discuss and report on.

Preparation

- Organize the students into groups of four.

WATER PARK DESIGN

Task: *You will work in a group to consider a task and report to the class about your group's discussion.*

❶ Find a group of four people to work with. Read the information below.

> **You are a group of designers who have been asked to design a new water park. The water park must have:**
> - five different water slides;
> - two pools (one must be suitable for toddlers);
> - a hair-raising "raft" ride for older children and adults;
> - a tube ride suitable for all ages; and
> - safety facilities.

The land you have available is shown below. Your design must fit around the features given above – they can not be removed.

❷ Discuss the ideas for each item in your group, making sure there are good reasons for where you decide to put each item and how it is built.

❸ Sketch your group's design for the park in the box below.

❹ Write notes about your design below.

_____
_____
_____
_____

❺ As a group, explain your design to the class.

TEACHERS NOTES   Water – Endangered sea animal

The multiple intelligence focus for this task is intrapersonal.

An intrapersonal student understands and analyzes his/her thoughts and feelings. He/She learns best through individual activities.

Indicator

- Researches to find information about an endangered sea animal.

Teacher information

- This worksheet requires students to work individually.

Answers

Answers will vary, but some information about the sea animals on the worksheet is below.

Humpback whale
- lives in the Atlantic and North Pacific oceans
- can grow up to 57 feet long and weigh about 22,000 pounds
- eats krill, plankton, and small fish
- predators are killer whales and humans
- endangered because until recent laws were passed, it was hunted for its meat, oil, and whalebone. Some countries still continue whaling.
- fewer than 10,000 left

Dugong
- lives along northern coastline of Australia and in warm shallow waters in the Pacific and Indian oceans
- can grow about 10 feet long and weigh about 880 pounds
- eats seagrasses
- predators are killer whales, crocodiles, and sharks
- endangered because of destruction of seagrasses due to pollution; gets caught in fishing nets; slow to reproduce; falls prey to killer whales, crocodiles and sharks
- fewer than 15,000 left

Kemp's Ridley sea turtle
- lives in Gulf of Mexico along eastern coast to Nova Scotia
- can grow to 24–27 inches long and weigh 70–110 pounds
- eats crustaceans, fish, and jellyfish
- predators like coyotes and racoons eat its eggs and animals like crabs and seabirds eat the hatchlings
- humans collect and disturb its eggs, gets caught in shrimp fishing nets, oil spills on feeding grounds, pollution
- about 3,000 left

Leafy sea dragon
- lives in waters around South Australia and Western Australia
- can grow to 11–17 inches long
- eats plankton and sea lice
- only known predators are humans (collecting them)
- endangered mainly because of water pollution
- numbers are not known

Preparation

- The students will need access to the Internet or resource books. To find information or pictures of one of the animals on the Internet, the students could type its name into a search engine.

Additional activities

- Design a poster that gives information about the endangered sea animal you wrote about. (visual–spatial)
- Challenge the students to do further research on their animal to find out what is being done to help it.
- Discuss how humans have affected the numbers of sea animals. In groups, students could create an action plan that outlines how we can be made more aware of how our actions affect sealife.

ENDANGERED SEA ANIMAL

Task — You will research information about an endangered sea animal.

An endangered animal is one that is in danger of dying out.
There are many endangered sea animals.

❶ Circle one of these endangered sea animals that interests you or choose your own.

humpback whale   dugong   Kemp's Ridley sea turtle   leafy sea dragon

❷ Research this animal using the Internet or other resources.

Name of animal

Draw the animal in the box.

Where does it live?

What size is it?

Circle the type of animal it is.

mammal   reptile   fish   other

What does it eat?

Does it have any predators? Name them.   Why is it endangered?

Approximately how many of this animal are left?

Why do you think it is important this animal is saved? _____
_____
_____

WATER – STUDENT SELF-ASSESSMENT

After completing this unit, I was able to …

word wise	rehearse and perform for an audience a shape poem for I have planned and written.	☆ ☆ ☆ ☆ ☆
logic wise	understand what makes water evaporate by evaluating observations during an experiment.	☆ ☆ ☆ ☆ ☆
nature wise	understand how animals and plants adapt to a lack of water.	☆ ☆ ☆ ☆ ☆
picture wise	plan and draw a picture based on given information.	☆ ☆ ☆ ☆ ☆
body wise	plan, present and assess a cooking demonstration with a partner.	☆ ☆ ☆ ☆ ☆
music wise	create and perform a soundscape in a group.	☆ ☆ ☆ ☆ ☆
people wise	work in a group to consider a task and report to the class about my group's discussion.	☆ ☆ ☆ ☆ ☆
self wise	research information about an endangered sea animal.	☆ ☆ ☆ ☆ ☆

What I learned

© World Teachers Press®

www.worldteacherspress.com

MULTIPLE INTELLIGENCES – Book 2

LIFE CYCLES

Informational text ☐   ☐ Plan a fitness program   *body wise*

word wise   Life cycle of a frog ☐   ☐ Jingle—How do you grow?   *music wise*

logic wise   Growing seeds ☐   ☐ Animal interview   *people wise*

nature wise   Our class pet ☐   ☐ Action plan   *self wise*

picture wise   The cycle of life ☐   ☐ Student self-assessment

What I know	What I want to know

Keywords

Name:	Date:

www.worldteacherspress.com

© World Teachers Press®

MULTIPLE INTELLIGENCES – Book 2

LIFE CYCLES OVERVIEW

Verbal–Linguistic

- Write a diary entry as if you were a tadpole or another creature of choice.
- Research to find out about the life cycles of unusual or endangered animals or plants.
- Complete a crossword puzzle or word search using words associated with life cycles.
- Order a series of events from an animal's life cycle.
- Deliver a speech that describes an animal's life.
- Write a poem about the life cycle of an animal.

- Write an autobiography, *My life so far*, as if you were a creature, outlining the changes you have experienced in your life.
- Write a fold-out book supplying information about the life cycle of a plant or animal.
- Keep a journal about observations of the life cycle of an animal or plant, such as a silkworm or a giraffe.
- Interview a creature about its life and how it feels about the changes it goes through.

Logical–Mathematical

- Research to find the patterns in common with different life cycles.
- Graph the average heights of people of different ages.
- Research to write notes about how an animal's life cycle can contribute to its vulnerability.
- Grow seeds and record changes.
- Make tangrams into shapes to represent parts of a life cycle of an animal or plant of choice.
- Record time frames of various stages of a life cycle.
- Calculate lifespans of particular plants or animals.

- Classify animal life cycles according to the length of time from beginning to adult.
- Categorize animals and plants according to characteristics of their life cycle.
- Create time sequence charts showing the stages of a life cycle; include titles and time frames.
- Predict the next stage of a life cycle of an obscure animal or plant based on prior knowledge of other life cycles.
- Order the stages of a life cycle of a chosen plant or animal.

Naturalist

- Observe an actual tadpole turning into a frog or a caterpillar becoming a butterfly in the classroom. Record observations.
- Grow flowers or vegetables in the school and record weekly changes.
- Go on an excursion to a river or pond to find creatures that live there. Identify the stage of the life cycle. Consider how they survive.
- Keep a classroom pet to study the life cycle. What are the needs of the pet at different stages?
- Investigate a variety of life cycles (e.g. people, plants, insects, animals, fish, reptiles).
- Investigate animals that hibernate during different stages of life.
- Compare environments and cycles of similar species; e.g. toads and frogs.
- Investigate natural processes (such as drought, forestfires, floods) which influence breeding and survival rates of a particular species.
- Write a pet care manual for looking after a kitten or puppy through to it becoming an adult.

Visual–Spatial

- Create a story map showing the life of a plant or animal.
- Create a drama piece that shows the changes in a plant's life.
- Use a video camera to create a time lapse film of a tadpole changing into a frog or a silkworm into a moth.
- Take weekly photographs of a plant growing.
- Use recycled materials to build a 3-D model to demonstrate an animal's life cycle.
- Draw life cycles of particular animals/plants in the form of a flow chart and label them.
- Create a "life cycle wheel" representing a particular animal or plant.
- Create a display of photographs from magazines or personal sketches of baby and adult animals or plants.
- Look through magazines to find pictures of people in one of the five stages of their life cycle (baby – child – adolescent – adult – senior).
- Create montages/collages of life cycles.

© World Teachers Press®

www.worldteacherspress.com

LIFE CYCLES OVERVIEW

Bodily–Kinesthetic

- Act out life cycles of various plants and animals.
- Mime life cycle changes for others to guess.
- Play leapfrog.
- Play traditional games using animal movements instead of regular movements.
- Create a short play or role-play representing danger to the particular plant or animal during a specific life stage.
- Make 3-D mobiles of the life cycle of a particular animal or plant.
- Play follow the leader, with the leader using movements of various animals at various stages in life.
- Play charades to guess animal or plant life cycles.
- Do daily fitness activities as a butterfly, caterpillar, tadpole, frog, baby bird, and so on.

Musical–Rhythmic

- Listen to nature sounds. Do animals make different sounds at different life stages?
- Show changes in a life cycle by using musical instrument to represent the different stages.
- Create a "frog chorus" using a variety of sounds.
- Develop dance movements or rhythms based on sounds and movement of plants and animals at different life stages.
- Consider the life cycle of a sea turtle. When the young turtles hatch, they must get to the water across many meters of sand. Find music to match this frantic journey of the turtles.

Interpersonal

- In a group, write a play script that shows the life cycle of an animal.
- Play drama games where the class acts as people of different ages.
- Work together to develop a poster to demonstrate a particular life cycle. Present to the class.
- Discuss findings/information on a particular species/life cycle of an animal or plant.
- As a group, watch the Disney film, *The Lion King*. Discuss what is meant by "the circle of life."
- Interview a caterpillar on how it is feeling about becoming a butterfly.

Intrapersonal

- Create a photo album (with captions) that represents your life so far.
- Compare how long humans live in comparison to other animals.
- Write your feelings about how humans have contributed to some animals becoming extinct.
- Research/Investigate a species threatened by a change in the food cycle (by pollution or development).
- Consider what humans can and can't do at certain stages of their lives. What are the wants and needs of babies/toddlers, etc.? What are the roles and responsibilities of adults/seniors, etc.?

LIFE CYCLES
INFORMATIONAL TEXT

The definition of a life cycle is: *the development of a living thing from conception through to the production of a new generation*

Animals

Some animals die when they reproduce, while others are able to keep reproducing through their life until they die.

Animals have different ways of reproducing, depending on their environment. Some animals produce live young (one at a time or many at a time), some lay eggs (that then need to be incubated), others incubate eggs internally and then lay them so they hatch soon after giving birth, while a few give birth to live young which then need to spend time developing.

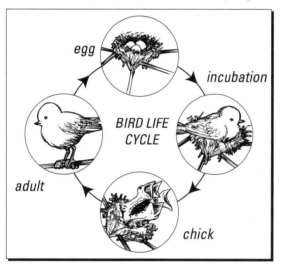

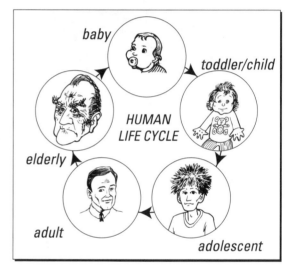

All animals change in size and shape as they grow and develop. Some animals change slowly, with small, gradual changes; e.g. mammals. Other animals change completely (metamorphosis) over a short space of time; e.g. caterpillars to butterflies or moths. Amphibians have three distinct stages to their life cycle—egg, larva (tadpoles for frogs), and adult.

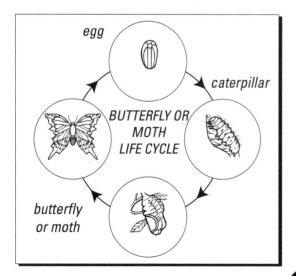

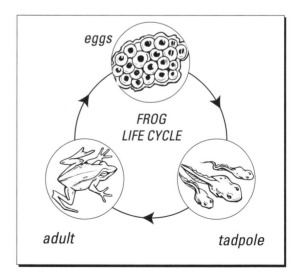

LIFE CYCLES
INFORMATIONAL TEXT

Some animals complete their life cycle in a matter of weeks, while others take many years. No matter how long it takes, it always follows the same pattern: growth and development and reproduction.

Vulnerability

At certain stages in its life cycle, an animal may be vulnerable. An example is that of a sea turtle which, as a newborn, must survive the trip across an open beach to reach the safety of water. At this time it is highly vulnerable to birds and other predators. This is one reason why a turtle lays large numbers of eggs.

Nature has provided protection to vulnerable species by ensuring large numbers of young are born, allowing for high rates of mortality. In addition to the pressures of nature, humans have, through their development, placed increasing pressure on many animal species.

The spread of population and the development of beaches have increased pressure on animals such as turtles, which normally return to the same beach to breed each season.

Plants

Plants can reproduce themselves from seeds, spores, or by using parts of the plant itself (e.g. stem cuttings). Most make seeds that can be dispersed by the wind, people, water, or animals. When the seeds have the right conditions to grow (space, food, water, light, temperature) they start to germinate.

Once the seedling starts to grow out of the seed it develops roots. The young plant continues to grow, developing a stem, leaves and, later, bearing flowers and fruits. The flower is the reproductive organ of the plant. Pollination of the flower leads to the making of more seeds and the cycle continues.

Non-flowering plants such as ferns and mushrooms reproduce through spores, usually found on the underside of the plant.

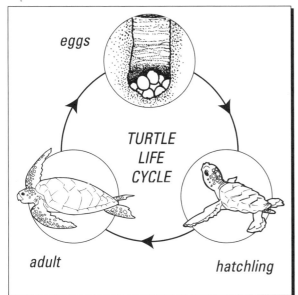

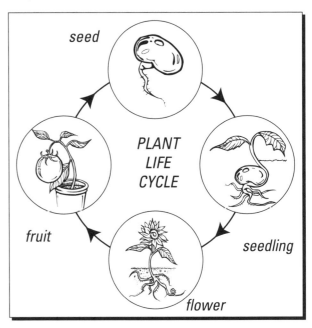

Teacher's Notes

Life cycles – Life cycle of a frog

The multiple intelligence focus for this task is verbal–linguistic.

A verbal–linguistic student thinks in words.
He/She learns best through activities involving reading, writing, and speaking.

Indicator

- Write a diary entry for each stage of a frog's life cycle from the point of view of the frog.

Preparation

- Gather samples of texts written in a diary style. Identify that diary entries are written in the first person and reflect the individual's personality.
- Make a copy of the frog's life cycle on an overhead transparency to display during the lesson.

Teacher information

- Display the life cycle of a frog on an overhead projector.
- Discuss the stages of development during the cycle.
- Encourage students to identify the way the frog may be feeling at different stages of the cycle. Brainstorm and record the "feeling" words on the board as a reference for the students.
- Discuss any challenges the frog may face at different stages of its life. What words could be used to describe how the frog feels about these? Record these words on the board.
- Students can then complete the diary entry for each stage of the cycle.
- Encourage students to share their diary entry with a partner.

Answers

- Answers will vary (Texts must be written in the first person to be authentic.)

Additional activities

- With a partner, write (using your diary entry as a starting place) and present a short play showing how a frog copes with the challenges of its life cycle and how it might feel at different stages. (interpersonal)
- Make a photo album of your life as a frog by drawing pictures showing your different experiences. (visual–spatial)

© World Teachers Press® www.worldteacherspress.com

MULTIPLE INTELLIGENCES – Book 2

LIFE CYCLE OF A FROG

Task: You will write a diary entry for each stage of a frog's life cycle from the point of view of the frog.

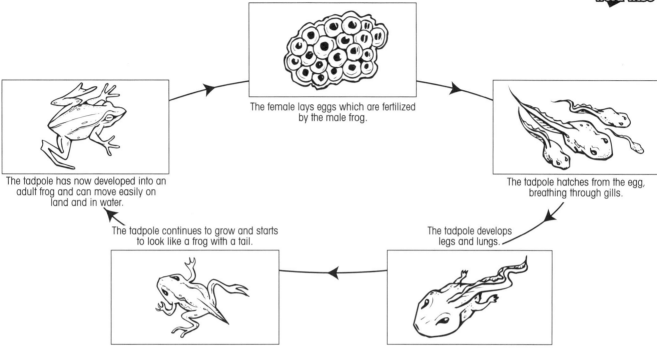

The female lays eggs which are fertilized by the male frog.

The tadpole hatches from the egg, breathing through gills.

The tadpole develops legs and lungs.

The tadpole continues to grow and starts to look like a frog with a tail.

The tadpole has now developed into an adult frog and can move easily on land and in water.

Write a brief diary entry as if you are the frog at each stage of the cycle.

The beginning of life _____
_____
_____

The developing tadpole _____
_____
_____

Adult frog _____
_____
_____

Female laying eggs _____
_____
_____

TEACHER'S NOTES

Life cycles – Growing seeds

The multiple intelligence focus for this task is logical–mathematical.

A logical–mathematical student thinks rationally and in abstractions. He/She learns best through activities involving problem-solving, numbers, and patterns.

Indicator

- Record observations showing how a plant changes as it grows.

Teacher information

- Display pictures of plants and encourage discussion to note the features of each. Students record their observations in note form. Pay special attention to color of foliage, foliage density, height, flowers or fruits, and so on.
- Discuss with students the types of things they might notice as their plants grow and change. Record on a chart the types of things students might observe.

Answers

Teacher check

Additional activities

- Display the results of the observation sheet in the form of a graph showing the growth of the plant over five weeks. (logical–mathematical)
- Compare the growth rate of different plants and identify if there were any causes for the differences. (naturalist)

Preparation

- Plant seeds for quick-growing vegetables such as tomatoes, runner beans, sugar snap peas, and so on. Allow time for shoots to appear before asking students to begin recording observations.
- Once recording begins, students should record observations on the same day each week.
- Students could share one plant between two or three but must record observations independently.

GROWING SEEDS

  Task — You will record your observations showing how a plant changes as it grows.

Plant Observations		
Date	Changes	Drawing
Measurement		
Date	Changes	Drawing
Measurement		
Date	Changes	Drawing
Measurement		
Date	Changes	Drawing
Measurement		
Date	Changes	Drawing
Measurement		

TEACHER'S NOTES   Life cycles – Our class pet

The multiple intelligence focus for this task is naturalist.

A naturalist student has an awareness of the patterns in nature. He/She learns best through activities involving animals, plants, and the environment.

Indicator

- Care for and observe a class pet and record any details of changes.

Preparation

- Introduce a pet to the class. It needs to be a young animal that will grow and change rapidly over about six weeks; e.g. baby chick, young tadpole, mice, silkworms, and so on.
- Students should have a roster of responsibilities, to ensure the pet is cared for and has everything it needs.

Teacher information

- Students can record their observations at random intervals, depending on any significant changes in the class pet.
- Observations should be made in note form and be as detailed as possible.
- As the animal grows and changes so will its needs. Students will be aware of these because of their involvement in caring for the pet. Record any changes.
- Drawings should be detailed and any major changes should be highlighted and labelled.

Answers

- Teacher check

Additional activities

- Class photos may also be taken as a record of the animal's life stages and how it changes. (visual–spatial)
- Use the Internet to further research your class pet's life cycle and record any details that may help you care and prepare for any changes to come. (verbal–linguistic)
- Record the changes of the class pet in the form of a time line. (logical–mathematical)

OUR CLASS PET

Task *You will care for and observe a class pet and record any details of changes.*

nature wise

Our class pet is a _____

I am responsible for _____

_____

Date:		Observations:
Drawing:		
		Needs:

Date:		Observations:
Drawing:		
		Needs:

Date:		Observations:
Drawing:		
		Needs:

www.worldteacherspress.com

55

MULTIPLE INTELLIGENCES – Book 2

© World Teachers Press®

TEACHER'S NOTES Life cycles – The cycle of life

The multiple intelligence focus for this task is visual–spatial.

> A visual–spatial student thinks in images, colors, and shape.
> He/She learns best through activities involving visualization.

Indicator

- Record the life cycle of a chosen animal in pictures.

Preparation

- Gather a number of resources for students to access in order to research the life cycle of an animal of their choice.

Teacher information

- Students will need to select an animal they would like to research for this activity.
- Research and take notes of the life stages of the chosen animal.
- Label and decorate Circle 1.
- The second circle has five divisions to allow for animals with more stages. If an animal has only three stages, leave two spaces blank.
- The students can then transfer their information onto Circle 2 using diagrams. Color.
- Cut out the circles and use a split pin to join them together in the center.

Answers

- Answers will vary

Additional activities

- Record the life changes of the chosen animal as a narrative. Present as a booklet, complete with artwork. Present to the class and establish a class library. (verbal–linguistic)
- Write a rap version of the life cycle of your chosen animal. Use instruments to make appropriate music and record onto a tape. (musical–rhythmic)

THE CYCLE OF LIFE

Task: *You will be able to record the life cycle of an animal of your choice in pictures.*

Circle 1:

1. Write the title; e.g. *Life cycle of a frog.*
2. Decorate to suit the chosen animal.
3. Cut along the dotted line.

Circle 2:

1. Draw pictures to show the life cycle of your chosen animal.
2. Color.
3. Cut along the dotted line.
4. Use a split pin to attach the circles together at the center point, with Circle 1 on top of Circle 2.

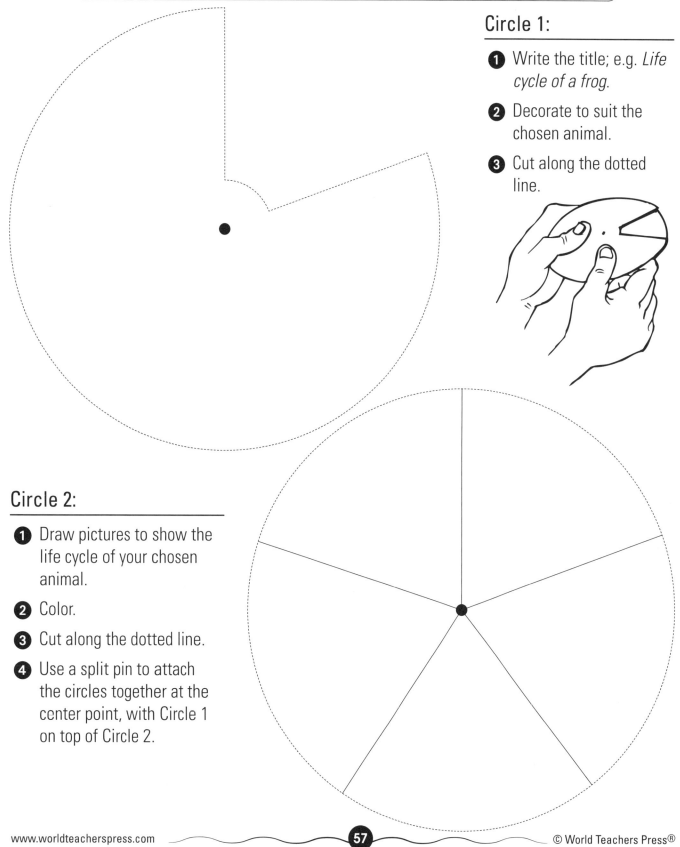

TEACHER'S NOTES

Life cycles – Plan a fitness program

The multiple intelligence focus for this task is bodily–kinesthetic.

> A bodily–kinesthetic student has good physical awareness.
> He/She learns best through "hands-on" activities.

Indicator

- Make a plan of a fitness program which represents the life cycle of a chosen animal.

Preparation

- Gather a number of resources for students to access in order to research the life cycle of an animal of their choice.
- Collect resources suitable for a fitness program; e.g. hoops, skipping ropes, balls, beanbags, cones, flags, and so on.

Teacher information

- Students will need to select an animal they would like to research for this activity.
- Research and take notes of the life stages of the chosen animal.
- As animals grow and change so do their movements; e.g. a baby goes from very jerky movements and not being able to control them, to being able to roll, grasp, crawl, and eventually walk.
- Students can work with a partner to discuss the movements made by their chosen animals at different stages. Students may like to physically mimic the movements to gain a better understanding of how the movement could be incorporated into a fitness program.
- Think about and record in a list the type of equipment required.
- Draw a simple flow diagram to show what will happen at each station.
- Students then set up their fitness program and demonstrate how it works to the class. Over the coming weeks, students could take turns running the morning the fitness session using their own fitness program.

Answers

- Answers will vary

Additional activities

- Make and record on tape a music composition which matches each station of the fitness program. This could be played while participating in the program. (musical–rhythmic)

PLAN A FITNESS PROGRAM

Task: You will make a plan of a fitness program which represents the life cycle of your chosen animal.

As animals change through their life cycle, their movements also change.

Your task is to choose an animal, research its life cycle and plan a fitness program which represents the changes of the animal through its life.

For example, in the case of the butterfly, the program could run as follows:

Station ❶: Form your body into a ball and roll along a track.

Station ❷: Stretch out along the ground and crawl like a caterpillar through hoops.

Station ❸: Climb into a sack and cover your whole body. Then grow out of the sack. Repeat five times.

Station ❹: Fly like a butterfly under and over a series of obstacles.

❶ Name of animal

❷ Notes about life cycle.

❸ Movements made by my animal.

❹ Equipment needed for my program.

❺ My fitness program.

❻ Now move through your fitness program. How well did it work?

poor — okay — great

TEACHER'S NOTES — Life cycles – Jingle—How do you grow?

The multiple intelligence focus for this task is musical–rhythmic.

> A musical–rhythmic student has an awareness of music and sound.
> He/She learns best through activities involving music or rhymes

Indicator

- Record a jingle to music which highlights the stages of development of a chosen animal.

Teacher information

- Allow students opportunities to listen to and discuss jingles on the radio and television. Identify the main components of successful jingles. They are short, catchy, and simple. A good jingle should remain in the listener's head for some time after hearing it.
- Students will need to select an animal they would like to research for this activity.
- Research and take notes of the life stages of the chosen animal.
- Consider musical instruments which would suit the different stages of the animal's cycle; e.g. the tinkle of a triangle might represent the butterfly taking off in flight for the very first time.
- Jingles are full of descriptive words. Brainstorm and record as many descriptive words for the animal as possible. Record them in the box as a reference for writing the jingle.
- Students then write and rewrite their jingle until they are happy with the end result.
- Allow students to practice their jingle with musical instruments before recording onto tape. It may take several attempts to get it to sound right. Students may need to assist each other with the sound effects and/or music when recording.
- Present the recording to the class.

Answers

- Answers will vary (Choice of instruments and words should suit the chosen animal.)

Additional activities

- Use the descriptive words from the activity sheet to make a crossword puzzle. Give to a partner to solve. (verbal–linguistic)
- Make "What am I?" quizzes about the different animals researched for the activity. Can other students guess the animal? (logical–mathematical)

Preparation

- Gather a number of resources for students to help them research the life cycle of an animal of their choice.
- Record a number of radio and television commercials which use jingles.
- Collect resources suitable for making music; e.g. rice shakers, drums, xylophones, triangles, symbols, recorder.

JINGLE—HOW DO YOU GROW?

Task: You will record a jingle to music which highlights the stages of development of an animal of your choice.

① Which animal will you use in your jingle?
_____

② Record notes about your animal's life cycle.
_____
_____
_____
_____
_____
_____

③ What type of instruments and sound effects will you use in your jingle?

④ List some descriptive words you could use in your jingle.

⑤ Write your jingle.
_____
_____
_____
_____
_____

⑥ Record your jingle, complete with music and sound effects, onto a tape recorder. Share it with the class.

TEACHER'S NOTES

Life cycles – Animal interview

The multiple intelligence focus for this task is interpersonal.

> An interpersonal student enjoys being in groups or teams.
> He/She learns best through activities involving working with others.

Indicator

- Work with a partner to write, answer, and present to the class a series of interview questions directed at and answered by a chosen animal.

Teacher information

- Allow students opportunities to listen to and discuss interviews held on the radio and on television. Identify the main components of a successful interview. The interviewer is prepared with a list of interesting questions. He/She listens to the responses and may change the line of questioning to suit.
- Students will need to select an animal they would like to research for this activity.
- Research and take notes of the life stages of the chosen animal.
- Remind students how they put themselves in the "shoes" of the animal when they wrote their diary entries. This will require the same skills. Humor can be used during the interview to develop the character of the interviewee.
- Record questions and answers.
- Practice the interview, asking and answering the questions, until both parties are happy with how the interview is flowing.
- Students may dress in costume to present their interview to the class.

Answers

1. Teacher check
2. Teacher check
3. Teacher check

Additional activities

- Write an autobiography as if you were the animal you chose to interview. (intrapersonal)
- Make a poster to advertise your up and coming interview to the public. (visual–spatial)

Preparation

- Gather a number of resources for students to help them research the life cycle of an animal of their choice.
- Record a number of radio and television interviews.

ANIMAL INTERVIEW

Task: You will work with a partner to write, answer, and present to the class a series of interview questions directed at and answered by an animal of your choice.

1. Work with a partner. One of you is the interviewer and the other is the animal being interviewed.

2. Select an animal and research its life cycle. Animal: _____

3. Write a series of interview questions directed to the animal about the changes it faces throughout its life. Write answers to the questions. You may use humor if you want to.

Question 1: _____
Answer: _____

Question 2: _____
Answer: _____

Question 3: _____
Answer: _____

Question 4: _____
Answer: _____

Question 5: _____
Answer: _____

4. Practice your interview and present it to the class. You may like to dress in costume.

TEACHER'S NOTES

Life cycles – Action plan

The multiple intelligence focus for this task is intrapersonal.

An intrapersonal student understands and analyzes his/her thoughts and feelings. He/She learns best through individual activities.

Indicator

- Work independently to devise an action plan to help a selected animal survive its life cycle.

Teacher information

- Students record the various stages of their animal's life cycle and identify the hazards faced at each stage.
- Students may then need an additional sheet of paper to brainstorm what humans can do to help the particular animal survive the hazard. Record best possible solutions on the worksheet but attach the brainstorming sheet to the back of the worksheet.

Answers

- Answers will vary

Additional activities

- Create a poster to inform the public about the hazards being faced by your chosen animal and how they can help. (visual–spatial)
- Organize regular visits to the habitat of your chosen animal to observe it in its natural environment and attempt to put your action plan into place. (naturalist)

Preparation

- Gather a number of resources for students to help them research the life cycle of an animal of their choice.

ACTION PLAN

Task — *You will work independently to devise an action plan to help a selected animal survive its life cycle.*

The life cycle of some animals makes their survival very difficult. This has combined with the threat posed by human development, leading to numerous animals becoming endangered. The sea turtle is one example.

The life cycle of a sea turtle

The sea turtle is a very fast animal when in the water. On land, the turtle is very slow. In the life cycle of a turtle, the female must leave the water and lay hundreds of eggs in deep nests in the sand. When the young turtles hatch, they must get from the nest to the water, across many yards of open sand. There are only eight species of sea turtle and they face extinction from many different directions.

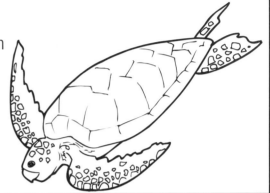

Select another endangered animal. Study its life cycle for possible threats and devise an action plan to help the animal in its quest for survival.

Animal:

Life stages	Possible threats	How people can help

LIFE CYCLES – STUDENT SELF-ASSESSMENT

After completing this unit, I was able to ...

word wise	write a diary entry for each stage of a frog's life cycle from the point of view of the frog.	☆ ☆ ☆ ☆ ☆
logic wise	record my observations showing how a plant changes as it grows.	☆ ☆ ☆ ☆ ☆
nature wise	care for and observe a class pet and record any details of changes.	☆ ☆ ☆ ☆ ☆
picture wise	record the life cycle of an animal of my choice in pictures.	☆ ☆ ☆ ☆ ☆
body wise	make a plan of fitness program which represents the life cycle of my chosen animal.	☆ ☆ ☆ ☆ ☆
music wise	record a jingle to music which highlights the stages of development of an animal of my choice.	☆ ☆ ☆ ☆ ☆
people wise	work with a partner to write, answer and present to the class a series of interview questions directed at and answered by an animal of our choice.	☆ ☆ ☆ ☆ ☆
self wise	work independently to devise an action plan to help a selected animal survive its life cycle.	☆ ☆ ☆ ☆ ☆

What I learned

© World Teachers Press®

www.worldteacherspress.com

MULTIPLE INTELLIGENCES – Book 2

FESTIVALS

Informational text ☐   ☐ Festival mask   *body wise*

word wise   Festival in the news! ☐   ☐ Rap it out!   *music wise*

logic wise   What's on? ☐   ☐ Festival day   *people wise*

nature wise   The environment celebrates too! ☐   ☐ Oh! What a feeling!   *self wise*

picture wise   What does it represent? ☐   ☐ Student self-assessment

What I know	What I want to know

Keywords

Name: Date:

www.worldteacherspress.com   67   © World Teachers Press®

MULTIPLE INTELLIGENCES – Book 2

FESTIVALS OVERVIEW

Verbal–Linguistic

- Identify similarities and differences among a range of festivals.
- Write diary entries describing what attending a particular cultural festival would be like.
- Write a list of things you would need to prepare, collect, or buy for certain festivals.
- Learn greetings or words from other languages that are associated with certain festivals.
- Compare how the same festival might be celebrated in different countries.
- Write a welcoming speech as the coordinator of a festival.
- Write a radio or television advertisement for a festival.
- Write a newspaper article about a fictitious festival.
- Role-play a roving reporter interviewing attendees of a festival.
- Brainstorm well-known festivals.
- Write about festivals held in other countries.
- Discuss festivals which members of the class celebrate.
- Research festivals and write specific information about each.
- Present a short talk about a festival in a particular country.
- Record an advertisement encouraging tourists to visit a particular country during a chosen festival.
- Write a newspaper report about a specific festival.
- Describe what it might feel like to be a performer at a festival.

Logical–Mathematical

- Classify festivals into categories such as the arts, sporting, cultural, etc.
- Complete logistical problems associated with planning a festival. For example, how much food is needed?
- Write a timetable of events for a favorite festival.
- Predict the best day in the month for a festival, given the weather patterns of the past few years.
- Graph the numbers of people attending a festival.
- Make a festival organizer's checklist.
- Organize a production line for making festival costumes – how can the costume-making be broken down into simple tasks?
- Given a certain number of volunteers, allocate suitable numbers of them to different tasks.
- Complete word problems involving numbers; for example, numbers of sequins needed for costumes, how many people will participate in a street parade?, how many buses are needed?
- Make a calendar of festivals.
- Budget for family and friends to celebrate well-known festivals such as Christmas.
- Calculate the percentage of a population involved in a particular festival.
- Make and measure a Chinese dragon created for Chinese New Year.

Naturalist

- Research festivals which have a nature theme.
- Invite as a guest speaker an organizer of a nature-themed festival to talk to the class.
- Use natural objects to create a poster to advertise a festival.
- Organize a scavenger hunt for natural objects for a festival.
- Investigate why certain festivals are held at particular times of the year.
- Consider the potential problems certain festival events may cause the environment and ways these problems could be solved.

Visual–Spatial

- Create a collage that shows the color and movement of a street parade.
- Create an advertising flyer for an upcoming festival.
- Design a festival logo to put on a T-shirt.
- Design a commemorative stamp that shows a popular festival.
- Take photographs at a local festival and arrange them in a photograph album with captions.
- Imagine you are a time traveler to an ancient festival. Recreate one of the events through art.
- Create a map with a key to show where festival events will take place.
- Design a series of articles to suit a particular festival; for example, hats, costumes.

FESTIVALS OVERVIEW

Visual–Spatial (continued)

- Paint a picture in crayons using color to show a fireworks display at a festival. Wash with black ink, runny black paint, or dye.
- Make a paper-mâché mask suitable for a festival.
- Create a Chinese dragon and perform with it.
- Make a map showing the route followed by a particular parade.
- Draw symbols or pictures that represent festivals. For example, a Christmas tree, star, or holly to represent Christmas and eggs, chicken, or a cross for Easter.
- Students make a pictorial record of information or details about a particular festival.
- Make a scrap book using photos and memorabilia from a particular festival.

Bodily–Kinesthetic

- Play charades, using the names of festivals discussed in the class.
- Make craft items that could be sold at a festival stall.
- Create a dance for a street parade or a class festival.
- Make some food that would be suitable to serve at a particular festival.
- Create props to be used for a "class" festival.
- Create tableus of festival scenes in small groups.
- Make masks and capes for characters in a festival procession.
- Play games relevant to particular festivals around the world.
- Learn dances relevant to a particular festival.
- Create a class mural of a festival students are learning about.

Interpersonal

- Perform group dances relevant to a particular festival.
- Using a given budget and price list, plan the catering for a festival in a small group.
- Role-play a group scene titled "Lost at the festival."
- In a group, discuss some ways money could be raised during a festival; for example, selling books, hot dog stand.
- In a group, brainstorm a list of suitable children's authors for a literature festival. Groups could also devise topics they think the authors should speak about.
- Plan, create, and present group activities that could be part of a drama festival.
- Design a poster to promote a festive occasion.
- Create a festival day. Plan and design how it should be presented.
- Follow a simple recipe to make food to be eaten during a particular festival.
- Prepare interview questions to ask representatives from different cultural groups about their celebrations.
- Choose one country and use the Internet and research center to investigate festivals and celebrations from that country.

Musical–Rhythmic

- Using the tune of a nursery rhyme, write suitable lyrics for a song about a popular festival.
- Choose suitable music for a street parade and explain your choice.
- Create background music to support an informative speech for a festival.
- Listen to music relevant to festivals in different countries.
- Learn dances and songs relevant to a particular festival.
- Identify how different cultures may use different types of instruments to make music for their festivals.
- Create background music and sounds using available instruments for specific festivals.

Intrapersonal

- Describe how you would feel to be chosen to take part in a particular festival.
- Detail the events you would include in a festival if you could organize a festival that celebrated YOU.
- Complete individual research on festivals on the Internet or by using encyclopedias.
- Describe any festivals you have been to or would like to attend.
- Share photographs from festivals you have attended.
- Make a collage to show feelings people might experience during a particular festival or festival event.
- Select a particular festival which has special significance and record personal details about it.
- Invent own festival with dances, food, purpose, music and costumes, etc.
- Keep a personal diary during a festival the student participates in.
- Speak to people in your family about festivals they have attended or are involved in.

FESTIVALS
INFORMATIONAL TEXT

A festival is a religious or other feast with performances of music, bright costumes, processions, exhibitions, etc. Festivals are often timed to coincide with some natural event, such as the beginning of spring.

Some festivals are looked at briefly below.

Diwali

Diwali is a five-day religious festival which occurs on the fifteenth day of Kartika. The celebration is often referred to as the Festival of Lights, stemming from the meaning of the word "Diwali." During the festival, homes are thoroughly cleaned, windows are opened and candles and lamps are lit to welcome Lakshmi, the goddess of wealth. Diwali is also a time to exchange gifts and prepare special meals.

Though variations exist throughout India, each day of the festival is dedicated to worshipping or acknowledging a different deity to bring positive values to people's lives, such as abolishing laziness, remembering the purpose of each day, removing anger, hate and jealousy, and seeing the good in others, including enemies. The festival of Diwali is as significant to Hindus as Christmas is to Christians.

Trung Thu

Trung Thu is a festival which celebrates the beauty of the moon and is held during autumn in Vietnam. People eat fish and flower-shaped moon cakes, with sweet fillings which are sometimes unusual, such as sugar with meat. Trung Thu is held from September to October.

Holi

Holi is another Hindu festival during which people remember the god Krishna, who loved to play tricks. One of his favorites was to drench his friends with colored water. On the morning of Holi, people wear old clothes and squirt colored water at each other with water pistols, pumps, or bottles. People get drenched—and very colorful! Holi is celebrated in March.

Shichi-Go-San

Shichi-Go-San is a Japanese festival which celebrates children who are three, five, or seven years of age. Children of these ages are thought to be lucky. Every child is given a long, narrow, decorated paper bag. After the family goes to pray at a shrine, the parents buy candy and toys to fill the bags. Shichi-Go-San is celebrated on November 15.

The Day of the Dead

The Day of the Dead, which is celebrated on November 1st and 2nd in Mexico are days for remembering relatives who have died. People build altars in their homes and visit cemeteries to decorate them with foods, candles, and colorful flowers.

FESTIVALS
INFORMATIONAL TEXT

Other well-known festivals held throughout the world include:

Shrove Tuesday

Shrove Tuesday (sometimes called Pancake Day) is held in February. It is celebrated in many countries on the day before Lent, the 40-day fast period before Easter. Long ago, people were not allowed to eat foods from animals during Lent, so on Shrove Tuesday foods like butter and eggs were used to make treats like pancakes.

Thanksgiving

Thanksgiving is celebrated on the fourth Thursday in November in North America. Thanksgiving is celebrated to remember early American settlers' thankfulness for their first harvest. People eat foods that the settlers would have eaten, such as turkey and pumpkin pies.

St. Patrick's Day

St. Patrick's Day is held on March 17. People wear something green to honor St. Patrick, who died long ago in Ireland. Many people also wear a shamrock, or three-leaf clover, which is Ireland's national emblem.

St. Lucia Day

St. Lucia Day is a Christian festival celebrated in Sweden on December 13. St. Lucia is the patron saint of light. A procession is held in which a young girl in a long white dress with a red sash wears a crown of candles. She represents St. Lucia. The five candles on the crown are burning. Some other girls walk behind as maidens. Carols are sung and lussekatt buns containing raisins are eaten, as well as gingerbread biscuits made into star and animal shapes.

Hanukkah

Jewish people all over the world celebrate Hanukkah, the festival of lights. It reminds Jewish people how, long ago, they won back their temple in Jerusalem. When the lamps were lit, it was found that there was only enough oil to keep them alight for one day. Instead, the oil burned for eight days. Hanukkah lasts for eight days, and a candle is lit each day on a candlestick called a menorah. Prayers are said before meals after each candle is lit and children are given a small gift each night. Families join together to eat latkes, which are potato cakes fried in oil.

Children's Day

Children's Day is celebrated in Turkey on April 23. This day is to honor children and the Turkish leader, Attaturk, the holiday's founder. All Turkish children dress up in national costumes or fancy dress. They go to a local football stadium and watch displays of children performing songs, dances, and poems. Afterwards, they eat kofte (meatballs) and burma (Turkish sweets) from the street stalls.

TEACHER'S NOTES

Festivals – Festival in the news!

The multiple intelligence focus for this task is verbal–linguistic.

A verbal–linguistic student thinks in words.
He/She learns best through activities involving reading, writing, and speaking.

Indicator

- Writes a newspaper article about a fictitious festival.

Teacher information

- Most reporters presenting a news article use the following format:
    – *Headline*
    – *Main detail*
        • Who?
        • What?
        • Where?
        • When?
        • Why?
        • How?
    – *Incidental/interesting detail*

    The news item tapers from the most important to the least important details at the bottom.

- Students should write the specific details about their fictitious festival on a sheet of paper before commencing to write their plan for their newspaper article. Headings could include the name of the festival, the date it is held, the reason for holding the festival, details about music, performances, costumes, parades, food, location, and crowd numbers.

Answers

- Teacher check

Additional activities

- Students use the same format to report on an actual community event or festival. Accompany the article with a photograph using the school digital camera.

Preparation

- Ensure students have some understanding of what a festival is. They should have some knowledge of the types of events that occur throughout a festival–performances, music, food distribution, costumes, processions or parades, and exhibitions. They should realize that most festivals are held to commemorate a specific idea, person, or event. These details will assist the students to write details about their own fictitious festival.

- Students will require pen/pencil or paper, and perhaps a dictionary, for correct spelling.

- Students should read and study the format of a number of newspaper articles before commencing this task.

FESTIVAL IN THE NEWS!

Task — *You will write a newspaper article reporting about a fictitious festival.*

1 Use the information you have written about your fictitious festival to plan your news report.

Headline

Main detail

Who?	What?	Where?
When?	Why?	How?
Incidental/interesting detail		

2 Events in order of occurrence.

(a) _____

(b) _____

(c) _____

(d) _____

3 Conclusion

_____

_____

_____

4 Use this plan to write your news report out neatly to present to the class.

www.worldteacherspress.com · 73 · © World Teachers Press®

MULTIPLE INTELLIGENCES – Book 2

TEACHER'S NOTES

Festivals – What's on?

The multiple intelligence focus for this task is logical–mathematical.

A logical–mathematical student thinks rationally and in abstractions.
He/She learns best through activities involving problem-solving, numbers, and patterns.

Indicator

- Completes a timetable for a festival he/she has attended.

Teacher information

- Students need to be familiar with the format of a timetable.
- Students should have a record of the events which occurred at the festival of their choosing.
- Students should be familiar with operations using digital and analog time.

Answers

1. Teacher check

Additional activities

- Create a timetable for the daily class activities for a week.
- Make a collage of a variety of timetables. Investigate the differences in design and format. Survey students as to favorites. Students explain reasons for their choices. (visual–spatial)

Preparation

- Students should have attended and recorded the events which occurred during the festival.
- Students should be familiar with the duration of the majority of the events or be able to make a reasonably accurate estimation of the time taken.
- Students should view and discuss a variety of different types of timetables before commencing this activity, including bus and train timetables, and programs for performances such as concerts.

WHAT'S ON?

Task — *You will write a timetable for a festival you have attended.*

1 Complete the information below.

Name of festival:	
Dates held:	
Event	**Duration**
(a)	
(b)	
(c)	
(d)	
(e)	
(f)	
(g)	
(h)	
(i)	
(j)	

2 Use the format below to complete a timetable of events for a specific festival you have attended.

Day and date		
Time	**Event**	**Location**

www.worldteacherspress.com

MULTIPLE INTELLIGENCES – Book 2

© World Teachers Press®

TEACHER'S NOTES

Festivals – The environment celebrates too!

The multiple intelligence focus for this task is naturalist.

A naturalist student has an awareness of the patterns in nature.
He/She learns best through activities involving animals, plants, and the environment.

Indicator

- Considers potential problems to the natural environment caused by holding a festival.

Teacher information

- Discuss large scale events students have attended and list any problems observed before, during, and after the event.
- Discuss the problems and list possible solutions.

Answers

- Teacher check

Additional activities

- Students invite the event organizer to speak to the class about problems relating to the use of the school grounds for such an event and how these problems are solved. (verbal–linguistic)
- Students listen to an officer from an agency such as a state conservation/land management authority speaking about public use of natural spaces.
- Collect magazine and newspaper articles about the use of particular environmental features to promote or hold sporting or cultural events.

Preparation

- Students should be aware that people and events organised by people may have a hazardous effect on the natural environment.
- Students should have attended a large scale event such as a football game, fireworks display, Christmas play, art and craft show, or school event before commencing this activity.
- Students scrutinize the school grounds to observe changes to the natural environment as a result of student, staff, and public use.

THE ENVIRONMENT CELEBRATES TOO!

Task: *You will consider potential problems to the natural environment caused by holding a festival.*

1 Read the newspaper report below and answer the questions.

Crowds Gather to Celebrate Festival

The Juice and Cheesemakers Festival this year was a big hit for both customers and producers

Picturesque Lyle River was the setting for the first annual Juice and Cheesemakers Festival held on April 17 and 18.

The venue, chosen from a number of prospective locations, proved an unexpected bonus for the organizers with many natural flora and fauna making appearances just in time for the festivities. Juice-tasters and cheese lovers in their thousands flocked to experience juices and cheeses offered by well-known and first-time producers. Singers, dancers, and musicians entertained the crowd, which included celebrities from the entertainment, literary, and sporting fields. Two such celebrities, Gina Wells and Daniel Biggs, presented awards to the producers of the most popular juices and cheeses.

2 What potential problems can you see being caused by holding a festival event in this setting? List them below and offer solutions.

Problem **1**	Solution
Problem **2**	Solution
Problem **3**	Solution
Problem **4**	Solution

3 On a separate sheet of paper, write about an experience when you have attended an event which had negative effects on the environment. Relate any changes that organizers could be expected to implement to improve the situation.

TEACHER'S NOTES Festivals – What does it represent?

The multiple intelligence focus for this task is visual–spatial.

> A visual–spatial student thinks in images, colors, and shape.
> He/She learns best through activities involving visualization.

Indicator

- Draws symbols or pictures that represent a particular festival.

Preparation

- Students should have read the informational text about festivals on pages 70 and 71 before completing this activity. These pages may need to be photocopied for each student or group of students to refer to.

Teacher information

- Students may choose any appropriate implement for drawing the symbols.
- Students may compare symbols at the completion of the activity. Answers will vary, since each student is choosing the symbol he/she thinks represents the particular festival.

Answers

- Answers will vary

Additional activities

- Students observe and draw symbols around the school or neighborhood and discuss their meaning.
- Students investigate different festivals around the world and draw appropriate symbols which other students try to guess.

© World Teachers Press® www.worldteacherspress.com

WHAT DOES IT REPRESENT?

Task: You will draw symbols or pictures to represent a particular festival.

1 Draw symbols or pictures which represent these festivals.

St. Patrick's Day
Children's Day
St. Lucia Day
Hanukkah
Shichi-Go-San
Trung Thu
Holi
Diwali

2 Write the name for a fictitious festival.

_____

3 Describe some reasons for holding the festival and some events held.

_____
_____
_____
_____
_____
_____
_____
_____
_____

4 Draw a symbol which represents this fictitious festival.

TEACHER'S NOTES

Festivals – Festival mask

The multiple intelligence focus for this task is bodily–kinesthetic.

> A bodily–kinesthetic student has good physical awareness.
> He/She learns best through "hands-on" activities.

Indicator

- Designs, makes, and evaluates a mask relevant to a particular festival.

Preparation

- Students should have read the informational text about festivals on pages 70 and 71 before completing this activity.
- Students should collect materials to make their mask after creating their design.
- Students should be familiar with some basic techniques for creating masks.

Teacher information

- Students should choose a festival and design a mask which relates to some aspect of the festival.
- A series of lessons should be allowed for making the masks.
- Students should make provision for messy work by covering tables with newspaper and using an old T-shirt or smock while creating their mask.
- Students should be allowed enough time to produce a quality art product.

Answers

- Teacher check

Additional Activities

- Students may build upon skills learned during this activity to create masks relevant to other festivals or themes.
- Students could wear their masks in a "street parade" for the remainder of the school.

FESTIVAL MASK

Task — *You will design, make, and evaluate a mask relevant to a particular festival.*

Use the festival informational text to help you design and make a character mask to wear during Diwali, Holi, Trung Thu, or the Day of the Dead.

Describe what your mask will look like.	Materials
Draw your mask design in the box.	

1. Use your materials to make your mask design.
2. Compare your mask to those made by other students.
3. Evaluate your mask and write any changes you would make next time.

www.worldteacherspress.com © World Teachers Press®

TEACHER'S NOTES

Festivals – Rap it out!

The multiple intelligence focus for this task is musical–rhythmic.

A musical–rhythmic student has an awareness of music and sound. He/She learns best through activities involving music and rhythms.

Indicator

- Completes and performs a rap.

Teacher information

- Many forms of performances are an integral part of a festival or celebration. Music and dances of all kinds can be incorporated into a festival program.
- Raps are a form of rhythmic chant. They are also known as street rhymes or hip hops and are related to jazz vocalization, where a lead voice sets up a rhythm and another voice or a group voice improvises or repeats the words of the lead voice. Lots of raps can be traced back to African music. Raps are now commonly accepted in the music industry and in street performances across the world.
- The easiest beat to accompany a rap is a 4/4 beat—1, 2, 3, 4, 1, 2, 3, 4, 1, 2, 3, 4 ...
- Body percussion involves creating a beat using various parts of the body such as clapping, snapping fingers, stomping, creating sounds using the mouth and hands, etc.
- Students should have viewed, listened to, or learned a number of raps before commencing this activity.
- Students should work in small groups of four or five to write and practice their rap with accompanying body percussion.
- Students may wish to take time to incorporate other movements to accompany their rap.

Answers

- Teacher check

Additional activities

- Perform the raps for the class. The amount of applause will be an indication of how successful the students have been at creating their raps.
- Practice and perform the raps at a school concert or to raise money for a charity or project at the school.
- Devise bright, "funky" outfits to wear while "rapping." (bodily–kinesthetic)

Preparation

- Collect a variety of raps for the students to listen to either by recording video clips or encouraging students to bring copies of their own from home. View and discuss the various aspects of a rap such as music with a strong beat, rhyming lyrics, and movements to accompany the rap.
- Provide a number of CD or tape players for groups to use while constructing their rap. (Students may be allowed to bring their own from home.)
- Ensure adequate space for groups of students to go to while creating their raps.
- Ensure students are proficient at keeping a rhythmic beat using percussion instruments or body percussion.

RAP IT OUT!

Task — *You will create and perform a rap.*

1 In a group, decide each student's role. Write your decisions below.

The lead voice is	
(i)	has chosen to
(ii)	has chosen to
(iii)	has chosen to
(iv)	has chosen to

2 Using scrap paper, construct a draft of your rap. Use the example below to help you. (Remember to keep to a 4/4 beat.) You may choose a topic relating to festivals or your own choice.

①　　　②　　　③　　　④
Festivals are cool; festivals are great!
①　　　②　　　③　　　④
Music and dancing; food on a plate
①　　②　　　③　　　④
Funky gear, awesome sights
①　　②　　　③　　　④
radical sounds and spiralling lights

Rap it out!!

3 Write your final copy below. _____

_____

_____

_____

_____

_____

4 Now that you have written your rap, spend some time to add appropriate body percussion as chosen by each student. (Note: These may change to others which may fit the rap better!)

5 Practice the rap and body percussion together and perform it for the class.

TEACHER'S NOTES　　　　　　　　　　　　　　　　　　　　Festivals – Festival day

The multiple intelligence focus for this task is interpersonal.

> An interpersonal student enjoys being in groups or teams.
> He/She learns best through activities involving working with others.

Indicator

- Plans a festival day in a group.

Preparation

- Students should be divided into groups of six either by teacher choice or their own choice.
- Discuss and record information about festivals, feasts, or other events which students have attended. This may be useful information for the students when completing their plan.
- List problems or aspects which must be taken into consideration during planning. These may include locations for specific activities, provision of food stalls and exhibitions, entry prices for certain events, timing of events, and provision of performers (including musicians, actors, puppet shows, and dancers at various venues and times).

Teacher information

- Students should keep their plans simple. Live performances should involve no more than two or three groups, especially if the performers are entertaining more than once during the day. Static exhibitions may number more than two or three, since these remain constant. Limit food and drink stalls to three or four.
- Students may find, as they plan, that there is a need to add or subtract events or activities.

Answers

- Teacher check

Additional activities

- Draw a location map to give to festival-goers to enable them to find their way around the festival easily. (visual–spatial)
- Write a timetable of events to be held at your festival. (logical–mathematical)

FESTIVAL DAY

Task: You will plan a festival day in a group.

What is the name of your festival?

Why are you holding it?

What events will you hold?	Who will organize each event?
Where will each event be held?	Which performers will you involve and how will you contact them?
What food and drink stalls will be there? Who will supply the food and drink?	What time will specific performances or events take place?

What charges do festival-goers need to pay and why?

TEACHER'S NOTES

Festivals – Oh! What a feeling!

The multiple intelligence focus for this task is intrapersonal.

> An intrapersonal student understands and analyzes his/her thoughts and feelings.
> He/She learns best through individual activities.

Indicator

- Writes a diary entry about being chosen to participate in a festival activity.

Teacher information

- Students should feel confident enough to write about their feelings without embarrassment.
- Students should include information such as the long hours of training they have completed, how long they have been learning or performing their specific act or skill, how parents, coaches and friends have supported them, and how they started the particular activity.
- Students should feel free to express feelings, whether positive or negative. Some students may never have performed for a live audience before and may be feeling apprehensive or nervous. Teachers should accept these feelings, as well as the fact that students may have experienced a mixture of positive and negative feelings in a similar situation in real life.
- Students may require a dictionary to spell unfamiliar words.

Answers

- Teacher check

Additional activities

- Students write a poem or story about a personal experience involving a similar situation.
- Students interview other students, teachers, or neighbors who have been through a rigorous selection process to be chosen for a specific activity, event, or team and report back to the class. (visual–linguistic)

Preparation

- Other class members who have participated in live performances or been chosen for a particular sporting team or event (such as representing the school in a district cross-country running event) may give a short talk about their experiences. Students may say how they feel after winning an award or competition. Others may relate the honor of simply being chosen to participate.
- Students should be familiar with writing a diary entry.
- Teachers and students may brainstorm and list a variety of different activities which the students could use in their diary entry.

OH! WHAT A FEELING!

Task: You will write a diary entry about being chosen to participate in a festival activity.

1. Use the story starter to write a diary entry explaining your feelings after being chosen to participate in a festival event.

When I arrived at class this afternoon, the other guys were babbling away, excitedly. I asked them what they were going on about and Josh said that we had been asked to perform at the Coolin Valley Festival.

Dear Diary,

Draw here

2. Draw an illustration in the box above to accompany your diary entry.

FESTIVALS – STUDENT SELF-ASSESSMENT

After completing this unit, I was able to …

word wise	write a newspaper article about a fictitious festival.	☆ ☆ ☆ ☆ ☆
logic wise	complete a timetable for a festival I have attended.	☆ ☆ ☆ ☆ ☆
nature wise	consider potential problems to the natural environment caused by holding a festival.	☆ ☆ ☆ ☆ ☆
picture wise	draw symbols or pictures that represent a particular festival.	☆ ☆ ☆ ☆ ☆
body wise	design, make, and evaluate a mask relevant to a particular festival.	☆ ☆ ☆ ☆ ☆
music wise	complete and perform a rap.	☆ ☆ ☆ ☆ ☆
people wise	plan a festival day in a group.	☆ ☆ ☆ ☆ ☆
self wise	write a diary entry about being chosen to participate in a festival activity.	☆ ☆ ☆ ☆ ☆

What I learned

© World Teachers Press®

www.worldteacherspress.com

MULTIPLE INTELLIGENCES – Book 2

GOOD HEALTH

Informational text .... ☐   ☐ .... An active life

Why drink? .... ☐   ☐ .... Jingle—Selling good health

Nutrition information .... ☐   ☐ .... Party menu

Health and the environment .... ☐   ☐ .... Food and my body

Healthy food posters .... ☐   ☐ .... Student self-assessment

What I know	What I want to know

Keywords

Name:	Date:

GOOD HEALTH OVERVIEW

Verbal–Linguistic

- List sayings that involve body parts; e.g. "It costs me an arm and a leg."
- Hold a debate on issues such as smoking and exercising.
- Role-play interviewing a part of the body. Find out what it likes/dislikes, etc.
- Keep a food and exercise diary for a week.
- Play "What am I?" games using body parts.
- Deliver a speech on "Amazing facts about …" (e.g. the brain.)
- Label the major bones of the human skeleton.
- Write yourself a letter from your hair.
- Investigate the body's five senses.
- Research to find information about the functions of specific body systems; e.g. digestive system.
- Investigate healthy lifestyles – food, water, exercise, sleep, relaxation.
- Write a poem about the dangers of junk food.
- Create a crossword about healthy food.

Logical–Mathematical

- Conduct taste tests, eye tests, ear tests. Include a hypothesis to guide the investigation.
- Design an eye chart.
- Observe physical reaction times of a partner and record the results.
- Write step-by-step instructions on giving first aid in specified cases; e.g. nosebleed, sprain.
- Organize a list of facts about blood.
- Look at simple optical illusions and try to create their own.
- Measure distances in hand spans and footprints.
- Graph eye color, hair color, or student height.
- Categorize foods as "healthy" or "unhealthy."
- Collect data on pulse rate before, during, and after exercise.
- List items needed in a first aid kit.
- Create a time line of their life.

Naturalist

- Compare the workings of the human body with those of other animals.
- Explore fingerprints.
- Find out why hair is straight or curly.
- Find out why we sweat, shiver, and hiccup.
- View pictures of early humans and compare with humans now.
- Investigate the effect of weather on bodily functions; sweating, shivering, etc.
- Visit a hospital or nursing home.
- Find a place in a natural environment where you feel at peace.

Visual–Spatial

- Complete a jigsaw of the human body.
- Produce a brochure about first aid techniques.
- Design a mobile suitable for a baby.
- Chart the route of blood flowing in and out of the heart.
- Create a life-size sketch of the body showing major organs.
- Design comfortable footwear for school.
- Draw a self-portrait using mirrors and a black marker.
- Create a collage representing a healthy eating guide.
- Create a cartoon showing the dangers of smoking.
- Research color blindness.
- Play visual memory games.
- Construct an eyesight testing chart and use it to check the vision of class members.

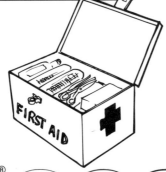

GOOD HEALTH OVERVIEW

Bodily–Kinesthetic

- Learn some yoga and Pilates moves.
- Complete an obstacle course on the playground.
- Lead a blindfolded partner around and discuss the experience of being blind.
- Write a list of action words and perform them in sequence.
- Do daily fitness.
- Create a dance involving the isolation of different body parts.
- Learn some sign language.
- Name the body parts involved in a series of simple movements.
- Role-play people who help us; e.g. doctors, dentists.
- Develop a dance/fitness program.
- Concentrate on exercises for particular body parts; e.g. arm curls, leg lifts.
- Use sign language and body language to communicate thoughts and feelings.
- Create a "health hustle" to popular music.
- Role-play first aid situations.

Interpersonal

- Plan an event at a local gym to encourage people to exercise regularly.
- Plan and construct a board game with a health focus.
- Plan and make a healthy lunch with a partner.
- As a group, plan a presentation promoting personal safety for younger students.
- Plan and present short skits to give other students strategies to deal with possibly dangerous situations.

Musical–Rhythmic

- Record rhythmic sounds to use for a rap such as hair brushing, clapping, tapping feet.
- Discuss how playing different music makes you feel.
- Observe a guest musician to discover what is really involved in making music.
- Use different body parts to make beats; e.g. clicks, claps, stamps.
- Find out how humans hear sound.
- Create movement patterns with the body in response to music.
- Watch a "one-man band." Which body parts are controlling the different instruments?

Intrapersonal

- Evaluate their own health habits; e.g. exercise, food.
- Draw a picture or create a collage to show the student's personality.
- Compare themselves to an animal, plant, or mineral.
- Describe the family member they most resemble. Describe the features they have in common.
- Set a personal physical fitness goal and record their success.
- Experiment to find out what happens when they exercise.
- Investigate a particular elite athlete.
- Research different diseases.
- What is personal space? Has someone invaded theirs? Suggest effective strategies to deal with this.

GOOD HEALTH
INFORMATIONAL TEXT

The most important nutrient you can put into your body is water. Although you can live several weeks without food, you can only survive a few days without water. This is because we constantly lose water through sweating, going to the toilet, and even breathing. The average person needs at least a half a gallon a day—half from drinks and half from food.

Many experts say that we should drink 6–8 glasses of water daily.

Foods contain different amounts of water. For example:

Food	% water	Food	% water	Food	% water
milk	87%	lettuce	96%	cookies	5%
apple	85%	cheese	37%	broccoli	91%
bread	35%	chicken	75%	butter	20%

Water fact file

Your body is made up of 66% water.	Water carries oxygen and nutrients through the body.
Your blood is 83% water.	Water gets rid of wastes.
Your bones are 75% water.	Water lubricates your muscles and joints.
Water stabilizes your body temperature.	Every system in your body uses water to work efficiently.

Diet

A well-balanced diet is made up of food from different food groups.

Food group	Provides ...	Important for ...
fruit and vegetables	vitamins, fiber, carbohydrates	managing weight, healthy bones, skin, red blood cells
dairy	calcium, protein, vitamins	energy, repairing cells, strong bones and teeth
bread and cereal	fiber, vitamins and minerals, carbohydrates, protein	energy, growth, repair of body
meat, fish, eggs, nuts	iron, zinc, protein	carrying oxygen in the blood, healing, growth

Junk food is too often high in sugar, saturated fats, and salt. It lacks nutritional value and can often cause people to feel sluggish and lack energy.

Obesity is a serious problem to which junk food contributes, particularly with children. Another factor is a lack of physical exercise.

GOOD HEALTH
INFORMATIONAL TEXT

Water pollution

Industry is one of the main sources of water pollution. It uses water and puts it back into the environment, sometimes containing chemicals, detergents, and other toxic materials. These pollutants can kill plants and animals and make the water unfit for human use.

Oil and rubber pollution from roads can wash into drains and fertilizers from farms and gardens can enter the underground water system, causing algae to grow in waterways.

Oil spills from supertankers carrying millions of gallons of oil are a major concern, as is untreated sewage pumped into waterways or oceans.

Smoking

Cigarettes contain over 4000 chemicals, many of which can cause cancer. Nicotine is addictive. Tar is a leading cause of throat and lung cancer.

Smoking can affect the following parts of the body	
lungs	cancer, breathing problems, asthma, emphyzema
heart	stroke, reduced oxygen, heart disease, high blood pressure, blood clots
stomach	ulcers
skin	dryness, wrinkles
mouth	cancer, stained teeth, gum problems, bad breath
hair	dryness, smell

Passive and active activities

Having a balanced lifestyle is very important if we wish to live a healthy life. We need to have time to be active, as well as time to relax and do more passive things.

One of the problems is that there are so many interesting activities available for us to do sitting down, that many people fail to be physically active enough to manage their weight, muscle tone, heart, and lungs. They also need to get more fresh air and sunshine. Fewer people walk or ride bikes to school or simply walk because it is easier to travel by car or public transportation.

The number of overweight adults and children is increasing because of our high fat and sugar diets and lack of regular physical exercise. This is worrying because obesity is an important factor in diabetes and heart disease, which are now seen even in younger people.

TEACHER'S NOTES   **Good health – Why drink?**

The multiple intelligence focus for this task is verbal–linguistic.

> A verbal–linguistic student thinks in words.
> He/She learns best through activities involving reading, writing, and speaking.

Indicators

- Understands the importance of water in maintaining health.
- Demonstrates understanding of the purposes and processes involved in writing expository text.

Preparation

- Collect and read "Letters to the editor."
- Discuss what the writers want the readers to do or think and decide if their arguments are persuasive.
- Discuss the differences between facts and opinions.
- An exposition is written to persuade people to think or do something. The writer states what he or she believes, lists arguments supporting this point of view, and finishes with a conclusion or summary.

Teacher information

- Encourage students to support their opinions with facts. Students can refer to the informational text about water on page 92.
- Expository texts often present opinions as facts. Encourage students' awareness of this as well as their ability to recognize the difference and understand what motivates this practice.
- Encourage students to edit and proofread their work.

Answers

1. (a) Water bottles
   (b) water bottles should be banned
   (c) Teacher check
   (d) Answers may vary
   (e) People are becoming dependent on water bottles.
2. Teacher check

Additional activities

- Make a collage of foods with a high water content, using pictures cut from magazines and glued to waterdrop shapes. (visual–spatial)
- Research causes of and efforts to overcome problems with the supply of drinking water in some countries.
- Tally glasses of water drunk each day for one week. Compare with other students. (logical–mathematical)

© World Teachers Press®   www.worldteacherspress.com

MULTIPLE INTELLIGENCES – Book 2

WHY DRINK?

Task: You will plan and write an exposition using your understanding of the importance of water for health.

WATER BOTTLES

Water bottles should be banned.

Everywhere I go I see young and not so young people sucking on water bottles. It seems that they can't manage a short bus trip, do their shopping, ride a bike, drive a car, or even have a conversation without drinking from a bottle.

The fad is most annoying and is an unnecessary waste of water. We managed very well for years with a drink in the morning, at night, and after strenuous exercise.

People are becoming dependent on these stupid bottles and it is time for them to be stopped.

Annoyed

❶ (a) What is the title? _____

(b) What does the author believe about water bottles? _____

❷ List three of the writer's arguments.

(a) _____

(b) _____

(c) _____

❸ (a) Which is the strongest argument? _____

(b) Did the writer state it first? _____

(c) What does the writer conclude? _____

❹
Exposition planning framework
Title
Problem/Point of view
Arguments (starting with the strongest)
Conclusion

Persuade "Annoyed" that drinking water is important for good health. On another sheet of paper, use the planning outline to organize your ideas. Then write your exposition in full, using strong, convincing arguments. Be persuasive.

TEACHER'S NOTES

Good health –Nutrition information

The multiple intelligence focus for this task is logical–mathematical.

> A logical–mathematical student thinks rationally and in abstractions.
> He/She learns best through activities involving problem-solving, numbers, and patterns.

Indicators

- Interprets nutrition information provided on food packaging.
- Compares different cereals for saturated fat, sugar, salt, and calories.
- Uses bar graphs to present and compare information.

Teacher information

- Food manufacturers are required to provide nutrition information because of increasing concern about healthy eating—diets low in saturated fat, sugars, and salt (sodium)—and body weight.
- Nutrition information can be difficult to understand and compare because serving sizes differ. Some labeling is misleading; e.g. "light" oil refers to color, not fat content, or calories.
- Students need to know how to present information on bar graphs.

Additional activities

- Compile a table of low and high saturated fat foods.
- Research the differences between saturated and unsaturated fat foods. (intrapersonal)
- Create a one-day healthy menu with a limit of 15 grams of saturated fat.

Preparation

- Students need to collect the nutrition panel from a cereal they usually eat.
- Graph paper is needed.

Answers

1. (a)   Cereal A –30 g   Cereal B –45 g
   (b)   The servings vary in size/weight.
   (c)   yes
   (d)   (i)   Cereal A
         (ii)   Cereal A
         (iii) Cereal A
   (e)   1540, 1520
   (f)   Teacher check (Cereal B has less sugars, total fat, salt and calories.)

2.

	Sugars	Total fat	Salt
A	35	4.0	270
B	20	3.0	190
C	Teacher check	Teacher check	Teacher check

3. None required

© World Teachers Press®

www.worldteacherspress.com

NUTRITION INFORMATION

Task: You will understand, compare, and graph information provided on nutrition information panels.

1 Compare these nutrition panels from different cereals.

Cereal A

NUTRITION INFORMATION
Serving size: 30 g (Approx. 1 cup)
Servings per package: 16

		Per serve	Per 100g
CALORIES		320	1580
PROTIEN	(g)	2.4	8.1
FAT	total (g)	0.9	3.0
	– Saturated fat (g)	0.2	0.5
CHOLESTEROL	(mg)	0.0	0.0
CARBOHYDRATE	total (g)	22.0	73.4
	– Sugars (g)	7.0	23.2
DIETARY FIBER	(g)	1.9	6.4
SODIUM	(mg)	80.4	268
POTASSIUM	(mg)	92.4	308
THIAMINE	(mg)	0.55 (50%)	1.83

Cereal B

NUTRITION INFORMATION
Serving size: 45 g (Approx. 1 cup)
Servings per package: 20.5

		Per serve	Per 100g
CALORIES		680	1520
PROTIEN	(g)	4.7	10.4
FAT	total (g)	1.3	2.9
	– Saturated fat (g)	0.4	0.9
CARBOHYDRATE	total (g)	30.8	68.5
	– Sugars (g)	9.1	20
DIETARY FIBER	(g)	4.3	9.5
SODIUM	(mg)	85	190
POTASSIUM	(mg)	185	410
THIAMINE	(mg)	0.55	1.22

(a) How many grams in one serving of:

(i) Cereal A? _____

(ii) Cereal B? _____

(b) Why is it difficult to compare servings of these two cereals?

_____

_____

(c) Do both companies provide information about 100 g of their cereals?

(d) Which cereal has the most:

(i) sugars? _____

(ii) total fat? _____

(iii) sodium? _____

(e) Energy is measured in calories.

Cereal A has _____ calories in 100g.

Cereal B has _____ calories in 100 g.

(f) Which cereal is healthier? _____

Why? _____

_____

2 Cut out the nutritional panel of a cereal you usually eat. (This is Cereal C.) Complete these bar graphs.

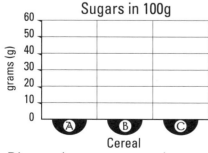
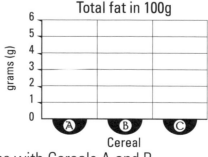
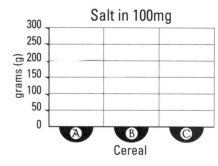

3 Discuss how your cereal compares with Cereals A and B.

TEACHER'S NOTES Good health – Health and the environment

The multiple intelligence focus for this task is naturalist.

A naturalist student has an awareness of the patterns in nature.
He/She learns best through activities involving animals, plants, and the environment.

Indicators

- Understands the health risks posed by air and water pollution.
- Proposes solutions to resolve these problems.

Teacher information

- Water pollution of both fresh water and salt water is thought of as one of the world's greatest problems affecting health. It is usually caused by humans. Industry is one of the main sources.
- Air pollution is mainly caused by smoke from factories and machinery, including motor vehicle exhausts.
- Possible solutions include: regulating industry, treating and recycling sewage, and using environmentally-friendly pesticides and biodegradable soaps and detergents.
- Refer students to informational text on page 93.

Answers

1. Answers may include:
   (a) car exhausts, industry, devegetation, wood fires
   (b) asthma, allergies, skin complaints, cancer, hay fever
   (c) Teacher check
2. Answers may include:
   (a) fertilizers, industry, salt, sewage, pesticides, detergents
   (b) Teacher check
   (c) Teacher check
3. Teacher check

Additional activities

- Many animals play important roles in maintaining people's health and well being. Choose an animal and describe its links to human health.
- Research an endangered animal. Describe the animal, where it is found, why it is endangered, why it is important, what is being done to protect it, and its connection with humans.

Preparation

- Discuss the relationship between humans and the environment and identify the three critical human needs—air, water, and food.
- Discuss what is meant by the term "pollution."

HEALTH AND THE ENVIRONMENT

Task — You will report on the causes and dangers of air and water pollution to health and propose possible solutions.

The environment is very closely linked to our health. We rely on the environment for air, water, and food.

Causes of air pollution
forestfires

❶ (a) Add to the list of air pollutants.

(b) List some of the health problems associated with air pollution.

Health problems

(c) Choose two sources of air pollution. Write notes to explain why they are dangerous to our health and what you think should be done to solve the problems.

Problem	Danger to health	Solutions

❷ (a) Add to the list of water pollutants.

(b) Which do you think causes the most serious health problem?
_____

(c) What do you think should be done about it?
_____
_____

Causes of water pollution
oil spills
chemicals

❸ Explain how pollution affects the food we eat.
_____
_____

TEACHER'S NOTES Good health – Healthy food posters

The multiple intelligence focus for this task is visual–spatial.

A visual–spatial student thinks in images, colors, and shapes.
He/She learns best through activities involving visualization.

Indicators

- Plans and creates a poster promoting healthy eating.
- Understands that posters are designed to persuade a target audience to think or do something.

Teacher information

- Students should be aware that to produce persuasive posters, they need to research factual, interesting information to include on their posters.
- They will need information on why we need to eat fruit and vegetables, dairy products, how many, how often, and possible consequences of an inadequate diet.
- Students can refer to the informational text on page 92.

Answers

- Teacher check

Additional information

- Make a collage of healthy food.
- Research osteoporosis. What is it? What causes it? How can it be prevented? (intrapersonal)
- Create a "danger" poster with food to be avoided.

Preparation

- Collects a wide variety of posters.
- Evaluate posters by asking:
  – Does it attract your attention?
  – Is it visually appealing?
  – How well is color used?
  – Is the message clear?
  – Is the message strong?
  – Is the message persuasive?
  – Who is the message for?
  – Is the written text appropriate?

© World Teachers Press® www.worldteacherspress.com

MULTIPLE INTELLIGENCES – Book 2

HEALTHY FOOD POSTERS

Task: *You will plan posters advertising fruit and vegetables and dairy food, and produce one of them.*

❶ Plan the content and layout of a poster to persuade young children to eat more fruit and vegetables.

Content	Layout
Special features to focus on	*Fruit and vegetables*
Which fruit and vegetables?	
Colors	
Written text (message, size, style, placement)	

❷ Plan a poster to persuade teenagers to eat more dairy foods.

Content	Layout
Special features to focus on	*Cow(s)*
Which dairy foods?	
Colors	
Written text (message, size, style, placement)	

❸ Choose one of the planned posters to make.

❹ Display posters and vote which:

(a) is the most eye-catching.

(b) has the clearest message.

(c) is the most persuasive.

www.worldteacherspress.com

MULTIPLE INTELLIGENCES – Book 2

© World Teachers Press®

TEACHER'S NOTES   Good health – An active life

> The multiple intelligence focus for this task is bodily–kinesthetic.

> A bodily–kinesthetic student has good physical awareness.
> He/She learns best through "hands-on" activities.

Indicators

- Mimes active and passive activities.
- Plans and demonstrates an exercise program.
- Reflects on ways to be more active.

Preparation

- Discuss why physical exercise is important for good health.
- Discuss some of the problems confronting those who do little physical activity; e.g. heart disease, diabetes, high blood pressure, circulatory problems, obesity.
- Students can refer to the informational text on page 93.

Teacher information

- Discuss the terms "active" and "passive."
- Fitness choices can be influenced by availability of resources, coaches, facilities, peer pressure, family history, finances, climate, interest, disability, medical factors, and role models.
- Role models can be a powerful influence on fitness choices. Ask students to nominate their sporting role models and discuss what they do and why they were nominated.

Answers

- Teacher check

Additional activities

- Plan and construct an obstacle course.
- Do a daily fitness session in the classroom and invite students to take turns to plan and demonstrate a section of the session, focusing on part of the body.
- Research to find the training schedule of an elite athlete. (intrapersonal)

AN ACTIVE LIFE

Task — You will mime active and passive activities, plan and demonstrate an exercise program and find ways to be more active.

There are many really interesting activities to do sitting down, but if we want to be healthy, most of us need to be more active.

1 (a) Make a list of passive and active activities you enjoy.

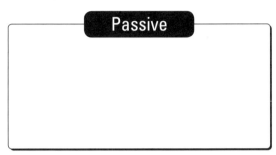

(b) If you could choose to do two new active things to do, what would you choose?

_____
_____

2 (a) Choose one active and one passive activity to mime for a partner. Which activities did you choose?

_____
and _____

(b) Was your partner able to recognize:

both ☐, neither ☐, or one ☐

of your mimed activities?

3 (a) Colin is a couch potato. He needs to be more active. Plan and demonstrate a 10-minute daily exercise program for him. He needs to exercise his arms, legs, and stomach muscles, but he doesn't want to leave the room.

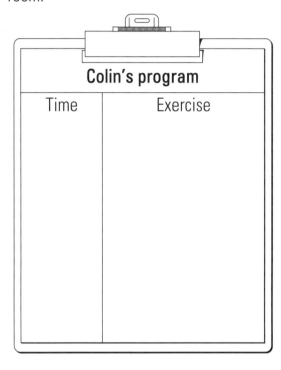

Colin's program

Time	Exercise

(b) Try Colin's program on a friend. Did he/she enjoy the program?

_____

Was your program hard work?

_____

4 How could you increase your physical exercise each day and enjoy what you are doing?

_____
_____
_____

TEACHER'S NOTES — Good health – Jingle – Selling good health

The multiple intelligence focus for this task is musical–rhythmic.

> A musical–rhythmic student has an awareness of music and sound.
> He/She learns best through activities involving music or rhymes.

Indicators

- Understands that music, rhythm and rhyme are used to enhance advertising messages.
- Writes an anti-smoking jingle and one to promote healthy eating.

Preparation

- At home, students listen to and watch musical advertisements selling food to allow them to participate in compiling a class list.
- Students stomp, clap, and snap the rhythms of these jingles.
- Students discuss the word "innovation" and understand that "text innovation" involves change and making new words.
- Students will need pencils/pens and paper for practice, as well as tape recorders.

Teacher information

- Text innovation – whole class, small groups and individual. Changing the words of familiar songs and jingles, retaining their rhythm and rhyme. For example:

  "Choose, choose, choose your food
  Be healthy every day
  Forget the pies and sausages
  Think fresh food – that's the way!"

- Students can refer to the informational text about smoking on page 93 to assist in writing their jingle.

Answers

1. Jack and Jill
2.–6. Teacher check

Additional activities

- Choose one jingle to adapt for television. Think about costumes, actions, setting etc.
- Research to find out when and why cigarette advertising was banned at sporting events. (intrapersonal)

© World Teachers Press® www.worldteacherspress.com

MULTIPLE INTELLIGENCES – Book 2

JINGLE—SELLING GOOD HEALTH

Task: You will change the words of a jingle to promote good health.

Text innovation

❶ Songs and jingles help us to remember words. Sing and clap this jingle. Which nursery song is the text innovation based on?
_____

> Bill and Ben went into town
> to buy a fat-filled burger.
> Bill ate his and felt so sick
> that he could walk no further.

❷ *Compose a jingle with an anti-smoking message using the same song. Sing and clap the words to keep the same rhythm.*

❸ Jingles are often used to sell particular brands of food. List some food advertised this way.

❹ Choose a food jingle and clap the rhythm for a partner.
  (a) Could your partner identify the product? _____
  (b) Is it a healthy food? _____
  (c) Change your jingle to advertise a *really* healthy food.
  _____
  _____
  _____
  _____

❺ Add sound effects or music to your jingle and record it.

❻ Change your jingle to advertise a different product of your own choice.

TEACHER'S NOTES   Good health – Party menu

The multiple intelligence focus for this task is interpersonal.

> An interpersonal student enjoys being in groups or teams.
> He/She learns best through activities involving working with others.

Indicators

- Works collaboratively in a small group to plan a healthy children's party menu.

Preparation

- Students need to know which foods are healthy and why and which foods to avoid and why (i.e. the dangers of a high saturated fat, high sugar diet).

Teacher information

- Some topics for class discussion could include:
    - What is junk food?
    - Why is it bad for you?
    - What are the dangers of a high saturated fat, high sugar diet? (heart disease, obesity, diabetes, etc.)
    - What makes food look good?

- Students would benefit from opportunities to discuss "What makes a good team member." Working cooperatively requires students to:
    - Listen politely
    - Take turns
    - Speak quietly
    - Think of good ideas
    - Keep working
    - Encourage others

- Students can refer to the informational text on page 92 for information about a healthy diet.

Answers

- Teacher check

Additional activities

- Debate the topic "Elementary schools should ban junk food."
- Plan and make a healthy lunch with a friend.
- Research the dietary needs of a diabetic. (intrapersonal)

PARTY MENU

Task
You will work in a small group (2 or 3) to plan a party menu for 20 children, with healthy choices which are tasty and look good.

1 Plan a party menu below with your group. Rate food, drinks and health on a scale of 1–5, with 5 being the best.

OUR BIRTHDAY PARTY MENU

Planned by:

Food	Health rating	Taste rating	Why it will look good
Drinks			
Finger foods			
Cold food			
Hot food			
Sweet food			
Birthday cake			

2 How well did your group work together? Rate each group member from 1–5 under the cooperation headings, with 5 being the best.

Name	Good ideas	Stayed on task	Listened to others	Spoke quietly

www.worldteacherspress.com

© World Teachers Press®

MULTIPLE INTELLIGENCES – Book 2

TEACHER'S NOTES

Good health – Food and my body

The multiple intelligence focus for this task is intrapersonal.

An intrapersonal student understands and analyzes his/her thoughts and feelings. He/She learns best through individual activities.

Indicators

- Researches information about different food groups, their functions and sources.
- Plans a daily menu which includes food from each group.
- Researches information on maintaining a healthy weight.

Preparation

- Students will need to be aware of different sources of information and how to access these, e.g. library, Internet.
- Provide for practice in note taking such as selecting and recording relevant information, keywords, and topic sentences.

Teacher information

- Students can refer to the informational text on pages 92–93.
- Ask students to reflect on how healthy their lifestyles are.
- When planning their healthy menu, students need to have some of each food type, but their menu also needs to include foods they enjoy and still be well balanced.
- Ask students to think about junk food. What is it? Why do children like it? What's good about it? What's bad about it?
- Ask students to complete the following sentence:
  "I eat junk food because …"

Answers

- Teacher check

Additional activities

- Write three personal goals that would help students enjoy a healthier life.
- Record the type and time spent on physical exercise for one week.
- List 10 things students like about themselves and one thing they would like to change.

FOOD AND MY BODY

Task — You will use information about different food groups to plan your healthy meals for a day.

The human body is like a machine. It works on the fuel it gets from the food it eats.

❶ Use this information to help you plan your meals for a day. Include tasty, nutritious food that you enjoy. Make sure you have sufficient protein, carbohydrate, fat, and water. Check the appropriate boxes for each meal.

Type of fuel	What for?	Foods to have
Protein	To help build muscles, organs, and glands and to help repair them.	meat, chicken, fish, eggs, nuts, dairy products, legumes
Carbohydrates	To supply energy to all the cells in the body and to produce glucose.	fruit, low-fat ice-cream, yogurt, breads, cereals, pasta, vegetables
Fat	Helps our body to stay warm, protects some organs, acts as a reserve tank of energy, helps keep skin and hair healthy.	meats, eggs, cheese, sometimes foods like chips and cookies
Water	Helps the blood to carry food to all parts of the body.	water

MY HEALTHY MENU

Meal	Food	Carbo-hydrate	Protein	Fat	Water
Breakfast					
Morning snack					
Lunch					
Afternoon snack					
Dinner					

❷ Research some do's and don'ts to help children to maintain a healthy weight. Write three of each on a separate sheet of paper.

GOOD HEALTH – STUDENT SELF-ASSESSMENT

After completing this unit, I was able to ...

word wise	plan and write an exposition using my understanding of the importance of water for health.	☆ ☆ ☆ ☆ ☆
logic wise	understand, compare, and graph information provided on nutrition information panels.	☆ ☆ ☆ ☆ ☆
nature wise	report on the causes and dangers of air and water pollution to health and propose possible solutions.	☆ ☆ ☆ ☆ ☆
picture wise	plan and produce posters advertising fruit and vegetables or dairy food.	☆ ☆ ☆ ☆ ☆
body wise	mime active and passive activities, plan and demonstrate an exercise program and find ways to be more active.	☆ ☆ ☆ ☆ ☆
music wise	change the words of a jingle to advertise good health.	☆ ☆ ☆ ☆ ☆
people wise	work in a small group to plan a party menu for 20 children with healthy choices which are tasty and look good.	☆ ☆ ☆ ☆ ☆
self wise	use information about different food groups to plan my healthy meals for a day.	☆ ☆ ☆ ☆ ☆

What I learned

© World Teachers Press®
www.worldteacherspress.com

DINOSAURS

Informational text .... ☐   ☐ Prehistoric fun and games

word wise

Lizard- and bird-hipped dinosaurs .... ☐   ☐ Dinosaur rap

music wise

logic wise

Dinosaur environments .... ☐   ☐ Theme party – Dinosaur style

people wise

nature wise

Dinosaur dig .... ☐   ☐ Dinosaur hunt

self wise

picture wise

Swinging dinosaurs .... ☐   ☐ Student self-assessment

What I know	What I want to know

Keywords

Name:	Date:

www.worldteacherspress.com

DINOSAURS OVERVIEW

Verbal–Linguistic

- Investigate and write a report on American dinosaurs.
- Imagine traveling back in time to the Jurassic period. Describe the dinosaurs you see.
- Using a comprehensive dictionary, find out the origins of dinosaur names (e.g. brontosaurus – "bronte" = thunder in Greek).
- Find dinosaur jokes on the Internet and tell them to the class or create a class booklet.
- Prepare an interview with a partner, role-playing talking to the last dinosaur that existed.
- Create a dinosaur dictionary.
- Write a review of a scene from the movie *Jurassic Park*.
- Write a newspaper article about a new dinosaur fossil discovery.
- Write a dinosaur poem using sound words.
- Read, research, and write a report about a specific dinosaur.
- Prepare a dinosaur quiz to give to the class.
- Write a conversation between two dinosaurs and perform it in front of the class.
- Give an oral report on a day in the life of a dinosaur, including relevant information.
- Keep a dinosaur diary from the dinosaur's point of view.
- Sort dinosaur words brainstormed by students into categories like sounds, characteristics, movements.

Logical–Mathematical

- Create a time line of dinosaurs and the period in which they lived; e.g. Triassic, Jurassic, Cretaceous.
- Create a dinosaur fact chart or a class *Did you know* booklet, organizing the facts into categories.
- Compare the sizes of different dinosaurs to animals that exist today.
- Create a code to solve dinosaur puzzles; e.g. Ask questions about a specific dinosaur and crack the code by solving number sentences (S = 23 – 17).
- Design dinosaur footprints on card and use them as an arbitrary measure for objects in and out of the classroom.
- Design symbols to show what particular dinosaurs are.
- Read about how the pterodactyl flew. Was it a true dinosaur?
- Use commercial dinosaur skeleton kits to construct models.
- Make observations about dinosaurs from pictures, tracks, or computer animation from a documentary.
- Compare a dinosaur to a lizard and a bird of prey.
- Research and develop a chart to compare lizard-hipped and bird-hipped dinosaurs.
- Identify dinosaurs from the Jurassic and Triassic periods from descriptions.
- Make dinosaur shapes from tangrams.

Naturalist

- Construct environments appropriate to the dinosaur era.
- Construct a life cycle showing the food chain of selected dinosaurs.
- Study the evolution of animals that were around in the time of the dinosaurs and which still survive today (dragonflies, crocodiles, cockroaches). How have they changed?
- Study the theory of climate change as the cause of the dinosaurs becoming extinct.
- Visit a museum to examine models or fossils of dinosaurs.
- Develop a list to show what would be needed to care for a "pet" dinosaur.
- Research dinosaurs of the land, bird-like reptiles, and swimming reptiles that lived in the Mesozoic era. Design a chart to show the differences.
- Investigate the job of an archaeologist.
- Compare the features of reptiles to four-legged dinosaurs and those of two-legged dinosaurs to birds of prey.
- Identify the physical features of different types of dinosaurs.
- Research to find how fossils are made.

Visual–Spatial

- Construct scale models of several dinosaurs.
- Create a dinosaur diorama with a prehistoric scene.
- Draw and label pictures of dinosaurs with relevant defensive parts and interesting features.
- Make simple fossils using shells, cleaned chicken bones, leaves, etc. pressed into plaster of Paris.
- Create a dinosaur cartoon character. Develop a simple cartoon strip using this cartoon character.
- Make dinosaur puppets (e.g. sock, finger, stick-puppets). Use them to perform a skit for the class.
- Make dinosaur footprints from a variety of animals and use these to create repetitive dinosaur art.
- Imagine you are riding on the back of a dinosaur. Describe what you can see.
- Design a dinosaur toy suitable for a baby.
- Create a story map to describe a narrative about a dinosaur.
- Paint a mural showing dinosaurs and their surroundings.
- Create a new dinosaur—model it out of clay or build it using recycled materials.

© World Teachers Press® www.worldteacherspress.com

MULTIPLE INTELLIGENCES – Book 2

DINOSAURS OVERVIEW

Bodily–Kinesthetic

- Create a scavenger hunt in a sandbox for students to find dinosaur "fossils."
- Participate in yoga or aerobics moves with a dinosaur theme.
- Create a moving dinosaur with a small group of people.
- Act out some dinosaur verbs; e.g. lumber, swoop, crash.
- Study dinosaur computer animation and describe how scientists think certain dinosaurs moved.
- Complete a "dinosaur obstacle course." (Hoops can be footprints, ropes as vines, etc.)
- Mold dinosaur shapes from a dough mixture and bake in the oven. Paint and display.
- Play "dinosaur tag" or "dodge" or adopt simple ball games.

Musical–Rhythmic

- Create a dinosaur dance.
- Learn songs about dinosaurs.
- Use musical instruments to make sounds to match how different dinosaurs moved.
- Make up song titles to suit different dinosaurs (e.g. *Brachiosaurus bump*; *Raptor rap*)
- Create rhythmic patterns of clapping, snapping, or stomping to suit different dinosaurs.
- Write a haiku poem about a dinosaur.
- Move as different dinosaurs to different pieces of music (e.g. slow, plodding music).
- Draw dinosaurs while listening to theme music from dinosaur movies.
- Listen to dinosaur movie music and comment on what action you think is happening.
- Record a "soundscape" to represent the times of dinosaurs.
- Clap out the names of different dinosaurs.
- View sections of dinosaur movies without the sound. Use instruments to create your own sounds.

Interpersonal

- In groups, research specific aspects of different dinosaurs (e.g. habitat, food, size, protective devices). Collate the information and report back to the class.
- View *Walking with Dinosaurs*. Discuss. Visit <http://www.abc.net.au/dinosaurs/default.htm>
- With a partner or small group, create and illustrate a dinosaur story suitable for a younger age group.
- Research areas of the world where dinosaur fossils and bones have been discovered. Mark and label them on a world map.
- What would it be like if dinosaurs were still alive today? Discuss and represent the group's ideas to the class.
- Create a model of a specific dinosaur (e.g. *Tyrannosaurus rex*) using only everyday materials
- Write a group script for a dinosaur play.
- Play a simulation game in which each member of a group role-plays a dinosaur expert with a theory on how the dinosaurs became extinct. Try to reach a group conclusion to the discussion.
- Play drama games with a dinosaur theme.

Intrapersonal

- Investigate theories of dinosaur extinction. Which do you think was the most likely?
- Investigate and read about known dinosaur stories/legends (e.g. Loch Ness monster).
- Design a pet dinosaur. What does it need? look like? eat? how does it move? Develop a list to care for it.
- Read nonfiction books or articles on dinosaurs during personal reading time.
- Research tools used on a "dig."
- Complete individual projects on a dinosaur, detailing its habitat, diet, movement, enemies, special features, etc.
- Write an action plan that shows what you would do to protect yourself from a dinosaur.
- Imagine yourself in prehistoric times and write a diary entry of a day in your life.
- Create a dinosaur cartoon character.

DINOSAURS
INFORMATIONAL TEXT

Dinosaurs lived over 65 million years ago during the Mesozoic era. The planet looked very different during the age of dinosaurs. The continents were much closer together. Some were even touching. The seas and lakes were warm and shallow enough for the dinosaurs to move from one place to another.

The word dinosaur means "terrible lizard." They were the largest animals to live on the earth. Some of the largest dinosaurs were Seismosaurus, Brachiosaurus, and Ultrasaurus. They were usually heavy, slow movers. Not all were huge, some, like Comsognathus, were small like a chicken and could move very fast.

Reptiles today are related to dinosaurs. They both have scaly skin and lay eggs. There were many different kinds of dinosaurs, but they didn't all live at the same time. As a group, dinosaurs ruled for over 165 million years. Each species, though, probably only lived for 4–5 million years at different stages through the Triassic, Jurassic, and Cretaceous periods. Some dinosaurs ate plants and were called herbivores. Others were meat-eaters called carnivores.

There are two main groups of dinosaurs:

(a) **Saurischians** or "lizard-hipped" dinosaurs. This group included:

Theropods (or meat-eaters) These were bipedal (walked on two feet), had small forelimbs, sharp teeth and claws (e.g. Allosaurus, Megalosaurus, Tyrannosaurus).	**Sauropods** (or giant plant-eaters) These were huge dinosaurs with long heavy necks and tails. They were thought to mostly walk on four legs (e.g. Apatosaurus, Diplodocus).

(b) **Ornithischians** or "bird-hipped" dinosaurs. This group included:

Plated dinosaurs with bony plates or spikes on their back or tail, a small jaw, and plant eating (e.g. Stegosaurus).	**Armoured dinosaurs** with bony plates and spikes all over their body and usually with a club-like tail (e.g. Ankylosaurus, Euoplocephalus).

DINOSAURS
INFORMATIONAL TEXT

(b) *continued*

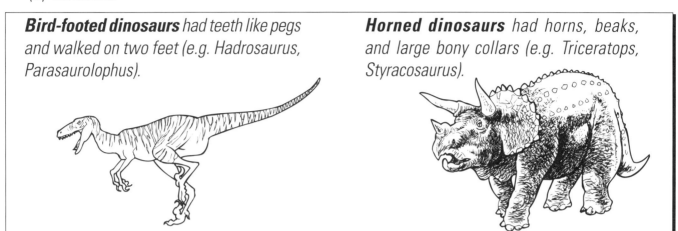

Bird-footed dinosaurs had teeth like pegs and walked on two feet (e.g. Hadrosaurus, Parasaurolophus).

Horned dinosaurs had horns, beaks, and large bony collars (e.g. Triceratops, Styracosaurus).

At least 700 different species of dinosaurs have been found, with even more probably to still be discovered.

Every year a new dinosaur is discovered by scientists around the world. No-one has ever seen a dinosaur as they mysteriously disappeared 65,000,000 years ago. We still know a lot about dinosaurs because of scientists called palaentologists. They uncover and study fossils, the remains of plants or animals found in the rocks of the earth.

When a dinosaur or prehistoric plant dies it can be eaten, rot, or be washed away. Only the skeleton may be left and over time this is covered in sand and mud. More layers of sand and mud cover the bones. Over a longer period of time, the skeleton becomes deeply buried. Thousands of years later, the bones become heavier and harder and become rock-like fossils. Wind and water wear away at the sand and mud, the layers disappear and the skeleton is exposed. When a fossil is found, scientists arc informed. A team of palaeontologists uses small drills and chisels to clean up the bones, carefully chipping away at the surrounding rock. The bones are cleaned and repaired very slowly in a laboratory. When a whole skeleton is found, it can be rebuilt and placed in a museum for us to view.

Dinosaur bones, teeth, footprints, skin impressions, and egg nests have been found in different places all over the world. Scientists study them and compare what they reveal with their knowlege of modern animals to help us understand and learn about the amazing prehistoric world of dinosaurs.

Scientists don't know why the dinosaurs became extinct. Some believe the climate of the earth became too cold and the dinosaurs died, or that the meat-eating dinosaurs killed so many that the remainder were not able to survive. The most popular theory, however, is that a meteorite hit the earth, covering it in a thick cloud of dust. This blocked the sun and caused huge, extremely rapid environmental changes to which the dinosaurs were unable to adjust.

TEACHER'S NOTES   Dinosaurs – Lizard- and bird-hipped dinosaurs

The multiple intelligence focus for this task is verbal–linguistic.

A verbal–linguistic student thinks in words.
He/She learns best through activities involving reading, writing, and speaking.

Indicator

- Researches a bird-hipped and lizard-hipped dinosaur to compare and complete fact boxes.

Preparation

- Discuss and have materials available (such as books and the Internet) for students to investigate bird- and lizard-hipped dinosaurs. Students may also refer to the informational text on pages 114–115.
- Discuss the variety of dinosaurs and their main differences (e.g. time of living; walk on four/two legs; herbivore/carnivore).
- Discuss the types of dinosaurs living in the Triassic, Jurassic, and Cretaceous periods.

Teacher information

- Every year, scientists discover new dinosaurs all over the world. Approximately 700 species have been named. Even though the dinosaurs existed for over 160,000,000 years, they did not all live at the same time; in fact, each species probably only lived for four to five million years.
- The dinosaurs are divided into two main groups called Saurischia (lizard-hipped) and Ornithischia (bird-hipped). Saurischia dinosaurs appeared in the Late Triassic period and were small meat-eaters like Coelophysis. New groups evolved through the Jurassic and Cretaceous periods, like the ferocious carnivores Megalosaurus and Tyrranosaurus. The first plant-eating saurischians could walk on all fours or on their hind legs, but these evolved in the Jurassic period to be much larger dinosaurs like Apatosaurus, which probably always walked on all fours.
- It is not certain when Ornithischian dinosaurs first arrived. The first were quite small and walked on their hind legs. They became larger during the Jurassic and Cretaceous periods like the "duck-billed" Parasaurolophus and Lambeosaurus. This group of dinosaurs also gave rise to the strange armored dinosaurs like Stegosaurus and Ankylosaurus. These armored dinosaurs were all plant eaters.

Answers

- Teacher check

Additional activities

- Make a list that sorts the dinosaurs into 'bird- and lizard-hipped' groups and their relevant subgroups. (verbal–linguistic)
- Make a time line showing the different dinosaurs and the period in which they lived (Triassic, Jurassic, Cretaceous). (logical–mathematical)
- Make up poems where students use alliteration to suit dinosaur names (e.g. All Albertosauruses ate apples). (verbal–linguistic)

LIZARD- AND BIRD-HIPPED DINOSAURS

Task: You will research and compare lizard- and bird-hipped dinosaurs.

Scientists have grouped dinosaurs into those with "birdhips" and those with "lizardhips."

Choose a dinosaur from each group to research and complete the table below.

Bird-hipped	Lizard-hipped
Name:	Name:
Where found:	Where found:
Plant eater or meat eater?:	Planteater or meateater?:
Length:	Length:
Height:	Height:
Weight (Mass):	Weight (Mass):
Period it lived: *Triassic Jurassic Cretaceous*	Period it lived: *Triassic Jurassic Cretaceous*
Interesting facts:	Interesting facts:

Discuss how the two dinosaurs are different.

TEACHER'S NOTES — Dinosaurs – Dinosaur dig

The multiple intelligence focus for this task is logical–mathematical.

A logical–mathematical student thinks rationally and in abstractions.
He/She learns best through activities involving problem-solving, numbers, and patterns.

Indicator

- Searches for fossils and records locations on a grid.

Preparation

- Fill plastic trays or kitty litter trays (enough for one per group) with clean sand. Number each group's tray.

- Place a selection of shells, dead leaves, dinosaur toys, dinosaur eggs (made from plasticine or modeling clay), chicken bones (boiled and dried to remove the meat), partially broken macaroni, or any other objects that may simulate those objects found in an archaeological dig. Make a note of objects hidden in each numbered tray to compare with student results on completion of the task.

- Discuss the role of palaeontologists. For fun, place a "Palaentologist at work—Please do not disturb!" sign on the classroom door. Explain how these scientists mark out a dig using a grid, and employ coordinates and very precise labeling to enable them to recreate skeletons or piece together a fossil's environment back at the lab.

- Each group will need to use the string or yarn and tape to make a grid across their tray, using the same coordinates as the worksheet. Determine which way the box goes and measure pieces of string that are at least 3 cm longer than the box dimensions.

- The worksheet enables students to accurately record where each object is found.

- Students take it in turns to use their digging tools (e.g. plastic forks, paintbrushes) in an up-and-down motion within each grid section to detect the fossils. (Students may wish to divide the grid by the number of people in the group.)

- When a fossil is found, the sand will need to be gently removed with the brush, so as not to disturb anything. The students number the objects as they are discovered and removed to a collection sheet. (Numbers can be written on paper and attached to each object with string.) Finally, they draw their object onto the grid and write its number and the person who found it underneath.

- When all objects have been found, the numbered objects can be totaled and compared to the teacher's total.

- Allow groups to discuss and share findings with class.

Teacher information

- Palaeontologists are fossil experts. Fossils are the remains of long-dead plants and animals. For a plant or animal to become a fossil, it has to have hard parts like bones or a shell. Jellyfish have no hard parts and so can not become fossils. A fossil can be formed in a number of ways: burial in mud and subsequent hardening; entrapment in tree sap; preservation in volcanic ash. A fossil is any evidence of life from the past. Most of the knowledge that scientists have gathered about the past has come from fossil imprints. Plants and animals leave their skeletons, a tooth, a footprint, or even an outline in dried mud. Bones are wrapped in plaster and imprints filled with plaster to create the shape of the original plant or animal.

Answer

- Teacher check

Additional activities

- Students bury their objects in different places and mark out a new worksheet of found fossils. (naturalist)

- Make their own fossils by pressing shapes such as leaves, shells and clean chicken bones in plaster of Paris and letting it set. (visual–spatial)

- Make pasta fossils by mixing potting soil ($1\frac{1}{2}$ cups) with several tablespoons of glue until the dirt holds together. Press out onto a greased plate or paper plate so it is about 1 cm thick. Gently break up some macaroni pasta in a zip-lock bag. Press the pieces into the soil to form a dinosaur skeleton. Brush white glue over the surface. Allow to dry and remove from plate. (visual–spatial)

DINOSAUR DIG

Task: You will search for fossils and record locations on a grid.

| **Teacher's Notes** | Dinosaurs – Dinosaur environments |

The multiple intelligence focus for this task is naturalist.

A naturalist student has an awareness of the patterns in nature.
He/She learns best through activities involving animals, plants, and the environment.

Indicator

- Uses picture clues to predict various dinosaur elements and environments.

Preparation

- Discuss the term "predict" and its meaning. Give simple visual/verbal examples of easily predictable situations for students to predict the outcomes (e.g. handle sticking off stove–could be knocked over; someone yawning–tired and bored).
- Discuss how scientists can use fossils to gather evidence of and knowledge about life from the past.

Teacher information

- A fossil is any evidence of life from the past. Most of the knowledge that scientists have gathered about the past has come from fossilised imprints. Animals and plants leave their skeletons, a tooth, a footprint, or even an outline in dried mud.
- Fossilized tracks are compared to those left by modern animals and scientists make educated guesses about how the dinosaur moved (e.g. big/small animals depending on the size; running –footprints further apart).

Answers

1. Teacher check
2. Possible answers
   (a) small dinosaur walking, larger dinosaur following further back
   (b) footprints mixed up – possible fight
   (c) only large dinosaur left – small one eaten, wounded, left behind or dead
3. (a) meat eater – long, curved, sharp tooth for ripping and tearing meat
   (b) plant eater – broad, flat tooth for grinding plant matter

Additional information

- Make fossil footprints using plaster of Paris. (visual–spatial)
- Make different-sized footprints out of card. Use these as an arbitrary measure for objects around the classroom or school grounds. (logical–mathematical)
- Research different dinosaur sizes and measure their actual lengths for comparison on a basketball court. (logical–mathematical)

DINOSAUR ENVIRONMENTS

Task   You will use clues to predict dinosaur environments.

We know a great deal about dinosaurs and the lands where they lived through fossils. Fossils can tell us about where the dinosaur lived, how hot or cold it was, what the plants were like, and what other animals lived at the same time.

1 What might these fossils tell you?

(a) 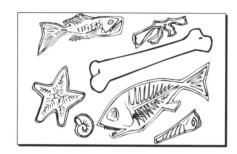 _____
_____
_____
_____

(b) _____
_____
_____
_____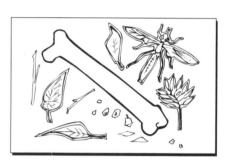

2 What story do these dinosaur tracks tell us?

(a) 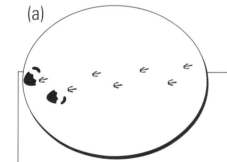   (b) 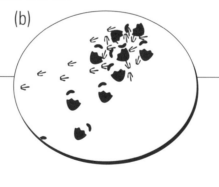   (c)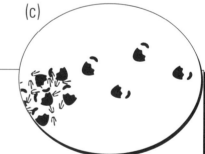

3 What type of dinosaur belonged to these teeth? Give a reason for your choice.

(a)

	meat eater	plant eater

(b)

	meat eater	plant eater

TEACHER'S NOTES   Dinosaurs – Swinging dinosaurs

The multiple intelligence focus for this task is visual–spatial.

> A visual–spatial student thinks in images, colors, and shape.
> He/She learns best through activities involving visualization.

Indicator

- Plans and constructs a dinosaur mobile.

Preparation

- Students will need these materials to work on their dinosaur mobile.

– paper	– crayons
– pencils	– paint
– lightweight card	– marker pens
– scissors	– colored pencils
– glue	– paper punch
– wire coat hangers	– heavy string or fishing line

- Students will need access to visual dinosaur resources (e.g. books, Internet videos, charts).

- Students plan their mobile choices on the worksheet.

- Select dinosaurs of a similar size in real life. Students may like to select a particular group of dinosaurs such as herbivores, carnivores, lizard-hipped, bird-hipped, ferocious, small, large.

- Students need to draw their dinosaur choices from sketches and plans onto paper (or directly onto card if they wish).

- Color or paint the shapes. (A combination may be used; e.g. paints/crayons)

- When dry, glue onto card (if only on paper) and cut around the dinosaur shape.

- Find the balancing point for each shape (see Teacher information). Mark the spot with a pencil and punch a hole.

- Tie string through each hole.

- Bend a wire coat hanger to make a shape to hang the dinosaurs from (adult help may be needed).

- Tie each dinosaur to the hanger. Have someone hold it while the dinosaurs are moved around the mobile until it is balanced. Tape or glue where the strings are tied so they stay in place.

- When dry, hang the mobile for display. Students could explain reasons for their dinosaur choices.

Answers

- Teacher check

Teacher information

- It may be best to confine student drawing to a set area for better balance (e.g. $\frac{1}{2}$ sheet of paper rectangles or slightly larger). It may be easier to have these already cut as their paper/card supply.

- To find a point of balance on their drawn dinosaurs, have students lightly hold each dinosaur by its top between their fingers. The balancing point will be when the dinosaur balances without tilting forwards or backwards. (Working in pairs might help here.)

- The coat hanger can be bent into any interesting shape that allows a point for four dinosaurs to hang at different levels. (Assistance needed)

Additional activities

- Create a dinosaur diorama. Research and plan dinosaurs from a set period or a group of "like" dinosaurs. Create a habitat for that era with pictures or drawings on the inside of a shoe box (e.g. plants, trees, volcanos). Draw or find pictures of dinosaurs that can stand up inside the box. Present the diorama to the class to explain selection choices.

- Design a new dinosaur. Where did it live? What did it eat? How did it protect itself? How big was it? Did it swim, fly, run, walk, crawl? What were its young like? Did it walk on two or four legs? Write a report about the new discovery then draw a large, bright picture to go with it. (verbal–linguistic)

- Make labels to accompany the students' mobiles and have them write a simple profile about each dinosaur they have chosen for display. (verbal–linguistic)

© World Teachers Press®   www.worldteacherspress.com

SWINGING DINOSAURS

Task — You will plan and construct a dinosaur mobile.

Use the boxes below to plan a dinosaur mobile using four dinosaurs.

Groups of dinosaurs I like …

My dinosaur choices …
1.
2.
3.
4.

Sketch plan of dinosaurs.

Colors

Colors

Colors

Colors

Coloring tool choices:

paint **pencils** **crayons** **markers**

TEACHER'S NOTES — Dinosaurs – Prehistoric fun and games

The multiple intelligence focus for this task is bodily–kinesthetic.

> A bodily–kinesthetic student has good physical awareness.
> He/She learns best through "hands-on" activities.

Indicator

- Develops a "dinosaur-themed" game from a known game.

Teacher information

- The purpose of a procedure is to deal with the general way to do things.
- A procedural text is composed of ordered sequences. They play a big part in our everyday life and are used in many contexts (e.g. recipes, science experiments, manuals for machines or appliances). Instructions for writing a game procedure could include:
  – How to win/goal of the game
  – Number of players
  – Equipment
  – Rules of the game
  – How to score

Answers

- Teacher check

Additional activities

- Demonstrate the games and allow other class members to participate, following the group's instructions.
- Make a class booklet of the "dinosaur-themed" games that the students have created. Add new ones to the book. (verbal–linguistic)
- Hold a "dinosaur sports" day/hour.

Preparation

- Play simple party games with students (e.g. pin the tail on the donkey, musical chairs, scavenger hunt, egg 'n' spoon race.)
- Discuss and list other games students know.
- Allow access to other resources on games.
- Work in small groups (4–5 students) for this activity.
- Ensure students have plenty of scrap paper and pens to plan their activity.
- Groups could present their final game procedure orally with the use of aids (e.g. equipment, chart) to the rest of the class.
- Allow students time to plan, test, and improve on their ideas before completing and presenting their finished game procedure.
- Have students brainstorm dinosaur words to do with size, shape, movement, or sounds in their group. These things may help them focus on the changes they need to make it a dinosaur game.

PREHISTORIC FUN AND GAMES

Task — *You will create and demonstrate a "dinosaur game."*

body wise

1 What party games do you know? Write them below.

2 Choose one of these games. Think about how you could change it to suit a "dinosaur theme."

Game chosen	Changes needed

3 Write a procedure to show others how to play the game.

Title:

Equipment:

Instructions:

4 Play the game following the instructions with your group. How do you rate it?

poor ☆ ☆ okay ☆ ☆ great

What do you need to change?

www.worldteacherspress.com

125

MULTIPLE INTELLIGENCES – Book 2

© World Teachers Press®

TEACHER'S NOTES

Dinosaurs – Dinosaur rap

The multiple intelligence focus for this task is musical–rhythmic.

> A musical–rhythmic student has an awareness of music and sound.
> He/She learns best through activities involving music or rhythms.

Indicator

- Plans, develops, and performs a rap.

Teacher information

- Raps are a form of rhythmic chant. They are also known as street rhymes or hip hop and are related to jazz vocalization, where a lead voice sets up a rhythm and another voice or a group voice improvises or repeats the words of the lead voice. Lots of raps can be traced back to African music. Raps are now commonly accepted in the music industry and in street performances around the world.
- The easiest beat to accompany a rap is a 4/4 beat – 1, 2, 3, 4, 1, 2, 3, 4 … . Body percussion involves creating a beat using various parts of the body, such as clapping, snapping fingers, stomping, and creating sounds using the mouth and hands.

Answers

- Teacher check

Additional activities

- Learn a dinosaur song and add movements to suit.
- Perform the raps for the class. The amount of applause will be an indication of how successful the students have been at creating their raps.
- Clap out the beat of dinosaur names.

Preparation

- Collect a variety of raps for students to listen to by recording video clips or encouraging students to bring copies of their own from home. These should be listened to and used at the discretion of the teacher.
- View and discuss the various aspects of a rap such as music with a strong beat, rhyming lyrics, and movements to accompany the rap.
- Provide a number of CD or tape players to use while constructing their rap (students could bring their own from home).
- Ensure adequate space for groups of students to go while creating their raps.
- Ensure students are proficient at keeping a rhythmic beat using percussion instruments or body percussion.
- Students should have viewed, listened to, or learned a number of raps before commencing this activity.
- Students should work in small groups of four or five to write their rap and practice it with accompanying body percussion.
- Students may wish to take time to incorporate other movements to accompany their rap.

DINOSAUR RAP

Task: *You will plan, practice, and perform a "dinosaur rap."*

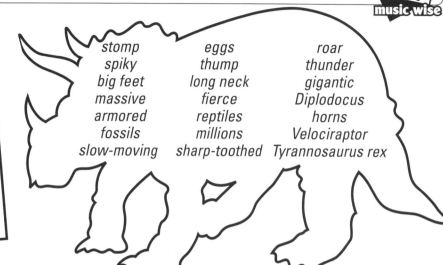

In small groups, create a dinosaur rap. Use some of the words alongside to help you. Think of rhyming words to dinosaur names, sounds, or movements. Add some words of your own.

stomp, spiky, big feet, massive, armored, fossils, slow-moving, eggs, thump, long neck, fierce, reptiles, millions, sharp-toothed, roar, thunder, gigantic, Diplodocus, horns, Velociraptor, Tyrannosaurus rex

❶ Plan your rap rhyme on scrap paper. Write your completed rap below.

_____
_____
_____
_____
_____
_____

❷ Create sounds and movements for your rap. Practice and, when ready, present your rap to the class.

Movement ideas	Music ideas

www.worldteacherspress.com

TEACHER'S NOTES

Dinosarurs – Theme party – Dinosaur style

The multiple intelligence for this task is interpersonal.

> An interpersonal student enjoys being in groups or teams.
> He/She learns best through activities involving working with others.

Indicator

- Works within a group to present a plan for a "Dinosaur Theme Party."

Teacher information

- Ensure students have had practice at working in groups. Emphasize the need for cooperation, listening to others, fair distribution of tasks, planning, organization, checking that all areas of the task are included, practice, and ordering for the overall presentation.
- Suggested group size of 3–4 provides students with the opportunity for greater success in communication, sharing of ideas, decision making, task completion, and overall presentation.
- Students will need access to a wide range of working materials (recycled materials, glue, paper) so a special corner or box of "goodies" may need to be organized prior to the lesson.

Answers

- Teacher check

Additional activities

- Write a class booklet of dinosaur jokes and riddles. (verbal–linguistic)
- Make a dinosaur paper-mâché model that could be used as a table decoration for a party or as a piñata. (bodily–kinesthetic)
- Build a huge dinosaur-like creature out of recycled boxes and materials. Invent a new dinosaur! (visual–spatial)

Preparation

- Expose students to a variety of resources dealing with parties, cake making, craft books, dinosaur books, and anything that may give inspiration to their plans.
- Working within groups, have students:
  - brainstorm ideas for all areas of the party,
  - allocate others within the group to develop one of those ideas (e.g. cake design) further,
  - present their research back to the group for final group decisions/approval,
  - present their part of the party plan in writing, using pictures or by showing created examples,
  - organize all the parts to present their "party theme" to the rest of the class—each person presenting his/her section.
- Ensure groups have access to scrap paper, scissors, glue, pens/pencils, card, or other materials they may require to complete and present their plan.

THEME PARTY – DINOSAUR STYLE

Task: *You will work with your group to plan and present ideas for a "dinosaur-themed" party.*

You have been asked to design a dinosaur theme party for children your age or younger. Brainstorm your group's ideas below.

Invitations	Costume/Hat ideas

Cake design	Party games
Songs to sing	

Dinosaur jokes/riddles	Decorations

TEACHER'S NOTES Dinosaurs – Dinosaur hunt

The multiple intelligence focus for this task is intrapersonal.

An intrapersonal student understands and analyzes his/her thoughts and feelings. He/She learns best through individual activities.

Indicator

- Researches dinosaur facts to suit a category.
- Identifies a dinosaur of interest to write about.

Teacher information

- The biggest dinosaurs were gigantic, small-headed, slow-moving plant eaters from the late Jurassic and Cretaceous period. Most had long necks counterbalanced by a huge tail. Some of the largest land dinosaurs discovered were *Argyrosaurus superbus* (65–130 ft), Diplodocus (90 ft), Brachiosaurus (85 ft) and *Supersaurus vivianae* (100–130 ft), but today's Blue Whale is bigger than any of these dinosaurs.
- The biggest carnivores were *Tyrannosaurus rex* (40–50 ft) and Spinosaurus (40–50 ft).
- The tallest dinosaurs had front legs longer than their back legs with long necks. Some were Sauroposeidon (65 ft tall), Ultrasaurus (65 ft tall) and Brachiosaurus (50 ft tall).
- The smallest fossils found belonged to Compsognathus (2 ft long, $3/4$ lb), Saltopus (2 ft long), Wannanosaurus (3 ft long) and a baby Mussaurus (14 inches long).
- The fastest dinosaurs were bird-like with slim, long hind legs and light bodies, such as Gallimimus, Ornithomimus, Coelophysis, and Velociraptor.
- The deadliest dinosaurs were fast moving, with huge claws, sharp teeth, and wing-like arms. These were Megaraptor, Utahraptor and Deinonychus.

Answers

(Note: Answers for this topic may vary slightly depending on the data sourced by students. Below are the more common findings.)

Try these websites for research:

http://www.prl.ab.ca/ab2001/records.htm

http://www.EnchantedLearning.com/subjects/dinosaurs/allaboutExtremes.html

http://pubs.usgs.gov/gip/dinosaurs/

Possible answers:

1. (a) Seismosaurus, Supersaurus, Ultrasaurus, Brachiosaurus
   (b) Compsognathus
   (c) Troodon (based on brain size to body size ratio)
   (d) Ornithomimids like Gallimimus, Struthiomimus
   (e) *Tyrannosaurus rex*, Gigantosaurus, Megaraptor, Utahraptor, Deinonychus
   (f) Anklyosaurus, Saichania, Stegosaurus
   (g) Muttaburrasaurus, Allosaurus, Rhoetosaurus, Minmi, Atlascopcosaurus, Leaellynasaura
2. Teacher check

Preparation

- Students will need access to a wide range of topic materials from which research facts (e.g. books, charts, Internet).
- Library times may need to be organized for students to work individually with resources.

Additional activities

- Make models of different categories of dinosaurs drawn from dinosaur facts found. Display with labels such as "*Tyrannosaurus rex* – fiercest dinosaur." (bodily–kinesthetic)
- Write a story about being the ... largest/smallest/fiercest ... dinosaur. (verbal–linguistic)

DINOSAUR HUNT

Task • *You will research and write about dinosaurs of interest.*

self wise

Use books and the Internet to find answers to these questions. Write another interesting fact about that dinosaur where possible.

1 Which dinosaur(s) was/were thought to be ...

Draw your dinosaur here.

(a) the largest?

(b) the smallest?

(c) the smartest?

(d) the fastest?

(e) the deadliest?

(f) the most armored?

(g) an American dinosaur?

2 Which dinosaur do you find the most interesting? Draw it and write some interesting facts about why you like it.

www.worldteacherspress.com

131

© World Teachers Press®

MULTIPLE INTELLIGENCES – Book 2

DINOSAUR – STUDENT SELF-ASSESSMENT

After completing this unit, I was able to ...

word wise	research and compare bird-hipped and lizard-hipped dinosaurs.	☆ ☆ ☆ ☆ ☆
logic wise	use clues to predict dinosaur environments.	☆ ☆ ☆ ☆ ☆
nature wise	search for fossils and record locations on a grid.	☆ ☆ ☆ ☆ ☆
picture wise	plan and construct a dinosaur mobile.	☆ ☆ ☆ ☆ ☆
body wise	create and demonstrate a dinosaur game with my group.	☆ ☆ ☆ ☆ ☆
music wise	plan, practice, and perform a dinosaur rap with my group.	☆ ☆ ☆ ☆ ☆
people wise	work with my group to plan and present ideas for a dinosaur theme party.	☆ ☆ ☆ ☆ ☆
self wise	research and write about dinosaurs of interest.	☆ ☆ ☆ ☆ ☆

What I learned

© World Teachers Press®   www.worldteacherspress.com

MULTIPLE INTELLIGENCES – Book 2

NOTES

NOTES

NOTES

NOTES

NOTES

NOTES